I0065250

'In fifty years' time this will be described as a seminal and transformative book. Today, some will see it as niche, bohemian or alternative. While the establishment is history, Simeon and his team are making it. If you are serious about engaging with the world and not skating over the top of it, read this book. Better yet – act on it.'
Tim Smit, co-founder of The Eden Project

'We live in a time when, as humanity, we face a choice: either we reclaim our birthright as citizens of Nature, and thrive together; or we continue to operate as consumers of Nature, and condemn ourselves to fighting one another to survive. To give Nature a voice and a vote is a simple and beautiful way for organisations of all kinds to make that choice. This book is essential reading for our times: a profound idea, beautifully communicated.'
Jon Alexander, New Citizen Project

'It started as a whisper with a tone of curiosity while reading the first page. The conscious reflection that "You could do this with your company" became ever more insistent as I read further. Simeon Rose has written a beautiful and generous book that may come to be seen as a significant landmark in humanity's rethinking of its relationship with the rest of the living world.'
Michael Pawlyn, architect and author of *Biomimicry in Architecture*

'Rose turns Nature from a passive victim into a bold board member. Imaginative and engaging, this book offers a fresh perspective on governance and genuinely makes you think differently.'
Katherine Tubb, UK Business and Biodiversity Forum and the University of Oxford

'Imagine how different the world would be if more people asked the simple question: "What would Nature do?". That's one of the powerful messages in *Nature's Boardroom*, a much-needed rationale for building and redirecting companies that are fit for the 21st century and beyond. Simeon Rose's clarity on how nature's wisdom can guide us to better business and life decisions is a truth-telling solution ready for a climate-impacted world.'
Leyla Acaroglu, Disruptive Design

NATURE'S BOARDROOM

Giving Nature a Voice and a Vote

Simeon Rose

BRISTOL
UNIVERSITY
PRESS

First published in Great Britain in 2026 by

Bristol University Press
University of Bristol
1–9 Old Park Hill
Bristol
BS2 8BB
UK
t: +44 (0)117 374 6645
e: bup-info@bristol.ac.uk

Details of international sales and distribution partners are available at
bristoluniversitypress.co.uk

© Bristol University Press 2026

DOI: 10.51952/9781529248265

British Library Cataloguing in Publication Data
A catalogue record for this book is available from the British Library

ISBN 978-1-5292-4824-1 paperback
ISBN 978-1-5292-4825-8 ePub
ISBN 978-1-5292-4826-5 ePdf

The right of Simeon Rose to be identified as author of this work has been asserted by
him in accordance with the Copyright, Designs and Patents Act 1988.

All rights reserved: no part of this publication may be reproduced, stored in a
retrieval system, or transmitted in any form or by any means, electronic, mechanical,
photocopying, recording, or otherwise without the prior permission of Bristol
University Press.

Every reasonable effort has been made to obtain permission to reproduce copyrighted
material. If, however, anyone knows of an oversight, please contact the publisher.

The statements and opinions contained within this publication are solely those of the
author and not of the University of Bristol or Bristol University Press. The University
of Bristol and Bristol University Press disclaim responsibility for any injury to persons
or property resulting from any material published in this publication.

Bristol University Press works to counter discrimination on grounds
of gender, race, disability, age and sexuality.

Cover design: Sean Knowles

For Nature

Contents

1   Lichen: Why This Idea and Why Now?   1

2   Moss: How Nature on the Board Works   15

3   Gorse: Guardianship and Speaking for Nature   29

4   Willow: Nature on the Board, Out in the Wild   45

5   Heather: A Cultural Shift   61

6   Bluebell: A Future with Nature at the Table   79

Index   95

1

Lichen: Why This Idea and Why Now?

A lichen is a mutualistic symbiotic association between a fungal partner and a population of unicellular or filamentous algal or cyanobacterial cells. ... Lichens are able to live in some of the harshest environments on Earth, and consequently they are extremely widespread. They occur from arid desert regions to the Arctic and grow on bare soil, tree trunks, sunbaked rocks, fence posts, and windswept alpine peaks all over the world. Some lichen thalli are so tiny that they are almost invisible to the unaided eye; others, like the reindeer 'mosses,' may cover kilometers of land with ankle-deep growth. One species, Verrucaria serpuloides, is a permanently submerged marine lichen. Lichens are often the first colonists of newly exposed rocky areas. (*Raven Biology of Plants*, 8th edition, Evert and Eichhorn, 2012)

Beginner's mind

'What if Nature really was the boss?' asked my creative partner (and wife), Anne Hopkins, in early 2021. Eighteen months later, in September 2022, Faith In Nature became the first company in the world to make Nature a director, giving the natural world a voice and a vote on all business decisions.

Faith In Nature is a natural personal care company that exists to make the best natural products (soaps, shampoos, conditioners, and so on) affordable for as many people as possible. The company was founded in 1974. A year earlier, Patagonia was founded. And only three years before that, 20 million people around the world came together for the first ever Earth Day – on 22 April 1970. Environmental consciousness was clearly on the rise and something was obviously stirring with new movements starting and a new generation of environmentally minded entrepreneurs setting out to do things differently. And yet, according to the latest World Wide Fund for Nature 'Living Planet Report', global wildlife populations have plummeted by 69 per cent since the year of that first Earth Day, and by an unbelievable 94 per cent in Latin America and the Caribbean. Here in the UK, we now have some of the lowest biodiversity in Europe and the Western world with the House of Commons Library estimating only 50.3 per cent remaining.

But we can't pretend this decline happened because we didn't know the direction of travel. While the sceptics argued about whether climate change was real or not, the rapid decline of the natural world has been plain to see. We've literally been recording the decline to the nearest 0.1 per cent. In that same time, the human population has grown 107 per cent and deforested land is up 40 per cent. Where was (the rest of) Nature meant to go? We've pushed the natural world to the margins, to the brink, and many species to extinction – threatening not only their existence, but the entire web of life. Instead of adapting our systems to allow for such dramatic change, we persisted with those same outdated systems, exacerbating the problem and continuing to ignore the needs and wants of the natural world. Business, of course, has been particularly guilty of this.

Much of this book speaks of giving Nature a voice. The truth, of course, is that Nature already has a voice. Nature has always spoken to us, through us and with us. Our books, galleries and museums are home to so many of those conversations, captured in folklore, art and myth. Did Nature really stop speaking with us as we became more 'civilised'? Or did we stop listening? Throughout my life, news reports have recounted Nature's cries. Nature has been screaming at us to open our eyes again, to open our ears, to change our ways. Through wind, fire and water, Nature has been warning us to stop. Instead we report isolated 'natural disasters' as if they are a series of events. Another catastrophe, rather than one ongoing natural disaster: ecological collapse.

But all of this is symptom, not cause. What we've been witnessing, really, is the breakdown of our relationship with the natural world. If we still saw Nature as family, as kin, as home, would we have allowed what's happened to happen? It seems we've replaced love and awe for detachment and indifference – reframing Nature either as an annoyance that must be controlled or as a resource from which the highest bidder can extract their profits. The price of that reframing is, of course, far greater than the highest bidder ever pays. All beings, us included, are poorer for it.

My own profession, advertising, has played a not insignificant role in this reframing. We've reduced people to 'consumers' and propagated the idea that happiness (or success, or peace of mind, or self-worth, or sex appeal, or, or, or ...) is whatever shiny new thing hits the shelves. And yet I've met many beautiful people in the ad industry. One of them is my wife, Anne. Many are among my closest friends. I didn't get into it because I loved capitalism. I got into it because I loved creativity. And weird as it might sound to some, I just loved *ads*. I love the puzzle of interrogating a brief to find something in it that somebody might actually care about, then finding a creative execution that speaks to them somehow. It might make them laugh, or nod along, or even rally against it – but it should provoke some kind of response. Advertising is about pushing buttons. What good advertising knows is how to make people care about something they didn't previously.

When Anne and I started working with Faith In Nature in 2016, we saw the privileged position we were in. It was an opportunity not only to grow awareness of the company, but to use the skills we'd developed throughout our careers to make people care about something we both cared deeply about, and something far greater: Nature itself.

But even finding the right language to talk about Nature is problematic, so I feel I should address a few points before going any further. When I capitalise the N in Nature, I sacrifice correct grammar for true meaning. I deliberately mean to elevate Nature from common noun to proper noun, to recognise Nature as an entity worthy of at least the same level of respect I would (grammatically!) show to even the worst, most undeserving, companies. For me, capitalising the N nods towards the ways more connected cultures might use 'Pacha Mama' or 'Mother Nature', names imbued with love and respect for our world – even though those names feel slightly uncomfortable in my mouth and can, when translated into Western culture, create division when what's needed is language that unites. It's worth saying too that although I speak about Nature as an 'it' or in such terms that make 'it' sound like 'other', I include all of us within that 'it'. There's just no elegant way to capture that sentiment with the tools the English language has given me.

Despite Anne and I spending most of our careers in the city, our roots were elsewhere. I'd grown up in the South Wales valleys, surrounded both by sights to make the heart soar as much as break – the lived reality of rolling green hills cut with black scars from decades of coal mining and the social difficulties that followed those mines' closures. Only half an hour north are the Brecon Beacons (now, as they once were, *Bannau Brycheiniog*) – a peaceful watercolour of a national park. Those hills are my happiest place, criss-crossed like the patchwork fields, with memories of some of my most loved, most cherished times.

Anne, meanwhile, grew up in the Barrington Tops – an Australian forest literally the size of Wales. Its endless waves of plunging landscapes, mostly unexplored, could devour the more modest Welsh hills I call home. The mountains are subtropical at their base and subalpine at their summit – and on a beautiful, isolated, farm among them sat Anne's home – edged by a river that is warm from the Australian sun at its surface and ice cold beneath.

Long before we made Nature a director, we both recognised Nature as a friend, a therapist, a collaborator, an artist, an inspiration, an extension of us and our families.

While neither of us have a background in environmental law, the Rights of Nature, corporate law, governance, policy, sustainability, environmental, social and governance (ESG) principles – or a whole load of other specialisms you might think important in appointing Nature to a company's board – our love for the natural world has always felt like enough. To echo the University of Derby's *Nature Connected Communities Handbook*:

> Research has found that our connection to Nature is much more important than our environmental knowledge in the actions we take to help the environment and wildlife. While people who feel close to Nature often know more about it than others who don't have a close relationship, knowledge and environmental education alone do not lead to Nature connection. How we interact with the natural world and feel about it matters more.

This feels intuitively true. Which is to say that we were left unmoved by so much of the 'climate conversation' happening. 'Climate' and 'the environment' were not what we'd grown up loving. Climate science is vital, but net zero targets, Sustainable Development Goals and ESG are not what set our hearts racing. So when we were brought in to rebrand Faith In Nature, what we saw was a creative opportunity to lead with the heart. What might we build if we put creativity and idealism front and centre? If we leapt heart-first?

We started by interrogating what was really at the core of the company and realised we didn't need to look much further than its (brilliant) name. But what did it really mean to have 'Faith' in 'Nature'? A brand is not just the way a company looks. It is the way a company acts, the way it behaves, its view on the world. None of this really starts in the marketing department or with a branding agency – it stems from the overall structure and management of the company. And so we got to thinking of organisational charts, redrawing the company's existing chart by moving everyone down a level and creating a new tier above them all: Nature. Now, no matter who sat at the 'top', Nature would always sit above them. This seemingly boring starting point is what unlocked so much of what came later. Then we wrote four words, large, across the boardroom wall: NATURE IS THE BOSS.

It encapsulated what was already in the air, but not yet articulated. It was a creative tool that helped reframe the way we thought about what the company was and what all of our roles were within it. Soon after, we put it to use when we turned to the brand's new visual world – creating a look that would carry the products from health-food stores to the mainstream. The natural aisles at the time were insipid and beige. Visually, 'natural' seemed to mean minimal and polite. But Nature was nothing of the sort! So we imagined that Nature, as boss, was the creative director and asked how the brand might look if Nature set the brand rules. That's why Faith In Nature now looks the way it does – wild, untamed and a riot of colour and pattern. Because that's exactly how Nature is. It was a fun thought experiment that led to a superficial change, but it also opened the door, and people's eyes, to looking at everything in a more ecocentric way. It brought a whole new meaning to the name 'Faith In Nature', a meaning that had been there all along, but was waiting to be uncovered.

A few years later, we were appointed to the board, and it was then that we saw the scale of this idea. Until that point, our focus had been design and messaging, pictures and words. But as directors, we needed to consider everything else a manufacturing company needs to consider. And sure, we had opinions. But, more so, we had realisations.

There, on the wall, were those four big words: NATURE IS THE BOSS. By then, it was written on the back of every one of the products too – so it was impossible to ignore – and the board was brought into this way of thinking. Still, the same topics would come up month after month as we'd discuss green initiatives, trying our best to act *as if* Nature was the boss – weighing up pros and cons that changed as often as market conditions. It required ecological thinking, accepting that Nature itself is always changing and what is in abundant supply one season is no longer available the next.

But we were also struck by something much more obvious. So much of this project comes from a place of creativity, of imagination and idealism. But also from common sense. It took a child to point out that the emperor wasn't wearing any clothes. And in the early days of this project, my mind often drifted to the Hal Ashby film, *Being There*, in which Peter Sellers' character, Chance the gardener, is a simple man who has never read a book and draws only from what he knows: TV and gardening. His advice is taken for mysticism. It isn't. It's obvious: 'In the garden, growth has its seasons. First comes spring and summer, but then we have fall and winter. And then we get spring and summer again.' Through his stating of the obvious, he eventually becomes a close confidant of the US president. In the film's final scene, he walks on water. He does all this because he doesn't realise he can't. To me, it is the most profoundly beautiful film.

Some of the most creative people I've met also have a habit of asking the most (seemingly) idiotic questions. This brilliant ability cuts the conversation down to such a basic level that instead of building upon shaky assumptions formed within a counter-productive set of rules, it's impossible not to start anew. And it was to such a basic level that things needed to be pulled apart when we realised the piece that underpins all this: every decision we make has an impact upon the natural world, yet the natural world itself has no say on any of these decisions. That is why Anne phrased her question the way she did. 'What if Nature *really* was the boss? What if Nature was our CEO?'

For over 20 years, we'd presented thousands of ideas, most of which ended up in the bin. Creativity becomes a bit of a numbers game in the end. You just keep churning out ideas, worrying less that they are 'good' or 'bad' and trusting instead that they will either be 'right' (for the time, client, brief, and so on) or 'wrong'. Who knows where ideas come from anyway? Easy come, easy go. But Anne has a brilliant brain and a huge, idealistic heart. She also has a particularly high hit-rate – and when she asked that question, I knew it was the most beautiful idea I'd ever heard. Sometimes, you do get an inkling.

The difficulty was knowing what to do with it. So we did the only thing we could: we waited for the answer to come to us. In time-honoured tradition, it came while sitting around a fire under a starry night. We mentioned the idea to our friend, Amy Wright, who'd previously worked in indigenous land rights in Australia. She mentioned great things happening in the Rights of Nature movement, of which we were becoming increasingly aware, and pointed us towards stories that blew our minds.

The Rights of Nature

The Global Alliance for the Rights of Nature defines the Rights of Nature as:

> the recognition that our ecosystems – including trees, oceans, animals, mountains – have rights just as human beings have rights. Rights of Nature is about balancing what is good for human beings against what is good for other species, what is good for the planet as a world. It is the holistic recognition that all life, all ecosystems on our planet are deeply intertwined. Rather than treating nature as property under the law, rights of nature acknowledges that nature in all its life forms has the right to exist, persist, maintain and regenerate its vital cycles.

I didn't need this spelling out to know that it was true. Nature's rights are inalienable. But I did need it naming to understand that this is more than just a philosophy or a belief system. It's an absolute colossus of an idea; a real legal movement that has the power to change our relationship with all life. And what I love so much about it is its inherent creativity. It's a piece of storytelling, just as our current understanding of rights is an outdated story. It's the retelling of a story from an entirely new perspective.

Imagine every story ever told from the perspective of a human (which is nearly all stories). Now imagine them, instead, written from the perspective of the natural world in which that human lives. It's an almost impossible task to imagine your own life story without you at its centre, but that's exactly what the shift from anthropocentric to ecocentric thinking asks.

Some countries, such as Ecuador and Bolivia, have already recognised the Rights of Nature at a constitutional level, showing that this is possible, it is real and it's happening. But even where those rights aren't recognised nationally, there are cases of individual aspects of the natural world having their rights recognised. And in some ways, in the short term, these make the idea more tangible. 'Nature' is so all-encompassing that it's overwhelming to reimagine everything at once. But reimagining a rights discourse, one aspect of the natural world at a time, is a more manageable step.

For me, I fall into this worldview simply through reflecting on my relationship with 'my' dog, Sonic. Of course, she is not 'mine'. She is her own being. She has her own needs and wants (which she makes clear) and she is as much a part of my family as I am her pack. Of course, I love her. And, of course, she has the right to 'exist, persist, maintain and regenerate her vital cycles'. In more everyday speak, she has the right to life, to joy, to health. She has the right to live fully in accordance with her own nature. And it's my duty to allow all of that. Millions of other people have similar relationships with others who are not human. The 'more-than-human'. And if we can step into such a relationship with one such being, why not another, and another? If Sonic has these rights, then surely so does the rabbit in the garden. And the jay in the oak tree. And why not the oak tree too? And the acorn that the jay carries to bury beneath the hawthorn on the banks of the stream, that flows to the river, that flows to the sea …

If humans are particularly good at one thing, it must be imagining. I find it much easier to imagine that another being has needs and wants as valid as my own than I do to imagine that no other being has needs and wants equal to mine. Imagination, combined with empathy, is what lets us trade places with all other beings. To ask how they might change the world if they could – and, recognising that they can't – to ask how we might change it on their behalf, to better serve all beings. Perhaps, in the web of life, that is what we are *for*.

So to find that the river Whanganui in New Zealand had been recognised as a fellow legal person was world-changing. This is what's known as 'environmental personhood' – a status that then enables the river to do such things as sue those who might pollute it. Or to advocate for its own 'right to exist, persist, maintain and regenerate its vital cycles'. Immediately this triggers the same logic I laid out earlier with Sonic, rabbit, jay, oak, hawthorn, stream and sea. Surely the health of the Whanganui relies on the health of all who rely upon it, who live in it or beside it. And where does the river begin and end? And why should the Rights of Nature begin and end there too? And if the Whanganui's rights are recognised, why not all rivers?

More to the point, if the frameworks exist to allow the natural world to speak in its own best interests, could those frameworks not be rebuilt within a company? Could Nature really be the boss? We were just connecting dots …

We followed the stories of the Whanganui to their source, searching for the types of lawyers who were writing these radical storylines. They led us to Grant Wilson of Earth Law Center in Colorado and, closer to home, Paul Powlesland of Lawyers for Nature in the UK.

Until that point, both organisations had looked to incorporate the Rights of Nature through governments, councils, national parks and other, bigger, bodies. Neither had looked to business for an ally, and neither had expected a business to call *them* asking for this kind of change. So to begin, there may have been some initial scepticism as the last thing either of them wanted was to attach their organisations to some kind of greenwashing stunt. But we were absolutely serious about doing this, and as that became apparent, ideas began to flow.

We decided early on that if we could arrive at a solution, that it should be open-sourced and freely available for any other business wanting to do the same. We'd gone beyond wondering whether Nature could be the boss of just Faith In Nature, and wondered instead how business (as a whole) might change if Nature had a voice and a vote.

If all this seems slightly bizarre, it is actually less bizarre than the current paradigm. As Paul put it to me early on, registering a UK company is as easy as filling in some forms and paying £50 to Companies House. Once that's done, this 'entity' – which is really an entirely imaginary thing – has a whole slew of legal rights assigned to it. But, say, the oldest tree in Britain – a yew in Perthshire – has no legal rights whatsoever. And it *exists*! You can sit under it, and ponder reality, as people probably have done for between 2,000 and 3,000 years.

Suddenly what seemed absurd a little while ago (a river as a person?!) seemed perfectly sensible. And now what seemed absurd was ... literally everything we accepted as normal. Anne and I have come to call these moments where the whole world gets turned upside down 'mind-flips'. And once they've happened, it becomes impossible to see the world again as you once did. Reality just keeps flipping, and flipping, and flipping ...

Something in the water

From first asking the question to Nature being appointed a director, 'Nature on the Board' (NOTB) took nearly 18 months to develop. We worked in a small team behind closed doors, never really allowing ourselves to believe we could make this work until it was absolutely guaranteed – which really became a reality once Brontie Ansell, Paul's co-director at Lawyers for Nature, got her teeth into it.

Once all was done and dusted, we prepared to announce it to the world on 14 September 2022. Unfortunately, on 8 September came the news that Queen Elizabeth II had died. Being a UK company, we decided to postpone our announcement until later in the month. What actually happened on 14 September was that Patagonia (a US company unaffected by the UK news cycle) announced they'd made Earth their only shareholder. Of course neither of us knew what the other was doing, but had it not been for a last minute change of scheduling, both Patagonia's story and ours would have dropped on the exact same day. Patagonia, founded just a year before Faith In Nature, announced how they'd recognised Earth as a stakeholder just a week before Faith In Nature did.

It was uncanny timing. And we couldn't have planned it better if we'd tried. Patagonia are, of course, pioneers in all sorts of ways. At the time nobody outside of the UK had even heard of Faith In Nature. So Patagonia created a huge wave of interest and we were in the right place at the right time to drop in with a story of our own. Instead of paddling against the tide, we were out in the surf together – and as true leaders do, Patagonia were among the first to reach out to show their support. Global media got in touch and we were launched into a conversation that exploded overnight. Earth as a shareholder? Nature as a director? What did it all mean? And were they the same thing?

They weren't. And having Patagonia's story to compare to our own allowed us to articulate the differences. What both approaches did was to look at the same problem, but through different ends of the telescope. Patagonia's model effectively means that all profits are given over to Earth (or the 'Holdfast Collective' – an entity responsible for distributing those profits) to counter climate change. And if a company's worth billions, that's serious. But what if a company's not worth billions? It's not the right answer, or even a viable solution, for nearly all other businesses on the planet. Instead, what NOTB does is ask *how* those profits are made, up-front. It brings Nature into the conversation before the decisions are made – so that better, more informed action can be taken. Rather than ask forgiveness after the event, it asks permission before it. And that's something all of us can do. All companies, no matter their size, can adopt a 'permission, not forgiveness' approach if they want.

So why is it that two companies that share so much in their DNA, but have followed two very different paths, should arrive at radical solutions at exactly the same time? My view is that it's simply inevitable. There really *is* something in the water. It's in the Whanganui. It's all around us. Nature hasn't stopped speaking to us, with us and through us. And some of us haven't stopped listening. I imagine Patagonia realised, as did we, that radical action is the only course of action still available to us. Another thing both companies have clearly done is to foster an environment where ideas like this can take hold, where idealism is celebrated and there is a restless maverick spirit.

Rewilding the boardroom

Imagine a boardroom, and I'm sure you'll see in your mind's eye much the same as I do. An artificially lit room, a table, chairs, a large screen and a group of directors turned to face each other rather than the windows behind them (if there even are windows). In that safe, sterile, space, those directors cannot see the people or the world their decisions impact. Those people, those places, are likely miles away. Maybe even the other side of the planet. It's much easier to destroy Nature when you cannot see the result of your decisions.

Rewilding is a process of ecological restoration aimed at increasing biodiversity in environmentally degraded, maybe even barren, spaces. And I cannot think of many more environmentally degraded, barren, spaces than most boardrooms.

But forests don't just grow in dead soil. 'Ecological succession' is the process where one plant community turns into another – it involves the arrival, extinction and changes in an abundance of different species. And it happens in stages. First come the pioneers, colonisers or early successional species, then the intermediate species, before finally the late successional, climax species. And where there is nothing, maybe just bare rock, lichens are often the first to move. Lichen can break down even bare rock into soil, drawing out the nutrients necessary for other organisms to take hold.

Perhaps that's what Patagonia and Faith In Nature really have in common; that they allowed the lichen in. For 50 years, the lichens have worked their magic until, finally, the rock broke.

And we can all be lichen, wherever we are.

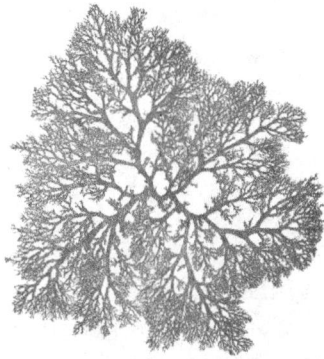

2

Moss: How Nature on the Board Works

Many species of mosses are found in relatively dry deserts, and several form extensive masses on dry, exposed rocks that can become very hot. ... Mosses are also the dominant plants on rocky slopes above timberline in the mountains, and a significant number of mosses are able to withstand the long periods of severe cold on the Antarctic continent. ... At about 3000 meters elevation on Mount Melbourne, Antarctica, the daily temperatures in summer mainly range from -10° to -30°C. In this incredibly harsh environment, botanists from New Zealand discovered patches of a moss of the genus Campylopus, where volcanic activity produces temperatures that may reach 30°C. The growth of Campylopus in this locality demonstrates the remarkable dispersal powers of mosses, as well as their ability to survive in harsh habitats. (*Raven Biology of Plants*, 8th edition, Evert and Eichhorn, 2012)

Why stop at lichen?

If you start thinking in terms of rewilding the boardroom – or rewilding the entire system – you start to see lichen at work everywhere. In fashion, in galleries, in architecture, in film, in books and throughout culture. And where culture goes first, business often follows. Increasing numbers of organisations are bringing Nature into their thinking, whether through Nature-positive language, developing Nature strategies, appointing Heads of Nature or greener governance models.

In ecological succession, no one species is more important than another. They are all co-dependent, part of a sequence of events. Lichen is no more or less important than a climax species, which, even if it's stood for thousands of years, can still be replaced by another. So if all these moves are implemented in the right spirit, then they are all intending towards the same, inevitable, outcome.

But succession isn't succession without a step change from one phase to another and our feeling was that we hadn't come this far to only come this far. Although the next phase for us was a legal one, it actually felt like another act of creativity – especially once we got the lawyers involved. Until learning of the Rights of Nature movement, I had little to no interest in the law. It seemed dusty and stuffy and a far cry from the creative career I'd pursued. But when it was explained to me that the entire rights discourse is really just a story – a collective agreement that benefits certain groups and entities over others – then it became apparent that to write a different ending was an act of storytelling. In these lawyers' hands, the law felt more like a creative tool.

A good story changes the way you see the world, the way the story of the Whanganui changed the way we saw the world. We wanted to create something that would flip other people's minds the way the story of the Whanganui had flipped ours. We wanted to push what was possible.

Fairly early on, we were advised that, legally speaking, Nature could not be the CEO of the company. But Nature could be a director. Our initial reaction was one of disappointment. It was a weaker headline. Wasn't it? About a minute later we realised it wasn't. It was actually far stronger this way. After all, even if we had made Nature the CEO, how many other companies would likely follow? In terms of a transfer of power, the vision of Nature as CEO is up there with Earth as the only shareholder. And two years after Patagonia made that move, no other companies have followed. Making Nature a director, on the other hand, feels like a smaller step – but has the potential to be far more wide-ranging. It's replicable. It's achievable. Every company can add another director to their board without ousting anyone already on the board. We wanted to prove that if we could do it, other companies could do it too. What change might we all create together?

This, to me, is a step change. When lawyers enter the frame to implement something radically different, something has shifted. We're past lichen and onto something new. Simple plants – like moss – can begin to take root.

At the end of this chapter is the open-source model that has been shared on Faith In Nature's website since day one. To date, it has been viewed 50,000 times and downloaded over 4,000. I have no way of knowing how many times it has since been shared or where it has spread. All I do know is that it has grown legs and developed a life of its own. Everyone involved with the project has also shared their learnings through public speaking, film, media interviews, podcasts and writing. The point of this book is to consolidate everything relating to Nature on the Board (NOTB) into one place so that the information is as freely available as possible. This isn't the sort of idea that should become 'management consultant-ified'. It should be shared, adapted, evolved, tweaked, refined and strengthened. But before that can happen, it needs to be understood.

When it is understood, one of the most common responses I hear to this idea is 'That's so simple, I can't believe nobody's done it before.' That's exactly what we felt when Brontie, Paul and Grant outlined it to us. I hope you feel the same at the conclusion of this chapter, or certainly at the end of this book. There is every reason not to stop at lichen. The main one is that succession doesn't stop. Even if Nature is not legally 'the boss', Nature still guides the whole process.

How Nature on the Board works

Before handing the reins of this chapter to Brontie, who wrote so much of the NOTB framework, I will explain in my words how it all works – which is really the acid test of how simple this idea is to understand. So much of the sustainability world's talk is incomprehensible to anyone outside the industry (and to some within it). This idea shouldn't be.

There are five key components to it:

1. *Purpose clause*

    A purpose clause was inserted into the company's articles. Many companies have 'purpose statements', but a purpose *clause* is a way of enshrining such sentiments into the constitution of the company itself. In our case, that purpose clause states that Faith In Nature exists for the benefit of the natural world.

2. *Guardianship model*

    Environmental personhood is the process of recognising the natural world, or aspects of it, as legal persons. So the Whangnaui is a legal person with its rights enshrined in constitutional changes – giving it the power to speak in its own best interest. But for a river – or Nature – to speak, legal guardians are needed to speak on its behalf. In the case of the Whanganui, its guardians are one member from the crown, and another from the Whanganui people. These voices combine to give the river a single voice. Likewise, at Faith In Nature, we have a rotating cast of guardians who speak together as Nature.

3. *Independence*

    Nature (or its guardians) is not employed by Faith In Nature as an employee. Nature is independent and external. Unlike, say, a Sustainability Director whose role it is to help the company achieve its targets in the most sustainable way possible, Nature has no vested interest in the targets of the company. Rather, Nature's role is to help all other directors see their choices through a Nature-first lens.

4. *An equal vote*

    Nature not only has a voice at the board, but an equal vote to all other directors. At Faith In Nature, there are currently ten directors, including Nature. Five of those are statutory directors, of which Nature is, again, one. Nature cannot veto a decision, and because Nature's vote is only one, Nature cannot force a decision through either – but neither can any director.

The overarching point here is that all other directors get to hear Nature's view before making their own decisions, so no director can be wilfully blind about the impact their decision will have upon the natural world.

5. *Transparency*

At the end of each year, the company must report back to Nature detailing all decisions made, its progress and, if it has chosen to act against Nature's wishes, to provide clear reason. Nature has the right to reply to this report, confirming that the report accurately describes the decisions and actions of the previous year. These reports are publicly shared.

The difficult questions

Whenever I speak about this idea, the same questions seem to get asked time and again. Sometimes I'm lucky enough to have Brontie beside me – meaning I get to pass all the most difficult questions to her. I'm going to do the same here.

Q. Talk us through your thinking. Was there an 'Aha! moment' when creating the model?

NOTB arose from a really important question: How can the governance of modern businesses and, more generally other institutions, genuinely bring Nature into their decision-making spaces, not just as a 'nice to have' or a tick box, but as an intrinsic voice within corporate strategy? More importantly, how would it look to begin to share power with Nature and really listen to what is good for Nature within the business space? There is a growing realisation that business really needs to be in service to all life on Earth and, of course, Nature more generally. We thought why not demonstrate that Nature could – and should – have a legitimate role in guiding the actions of companies, especially given the existential risks that environmental neglect poses to long-term business viability? This wasn't just an eco-conscious proposal; it was a strategic movement that recognised Nature as central to sustainable business success, and of course by sustainable we really do mean sustainable for all life on Earth. After all, the greatest subsidy a business receives is the service of Nature. The NOTB model was built with the pre-existing legal principle that directors are duty-bound to promote the success of the company. Traditionally, this has meant enhancing value for capital providers. Some take this very literally of course, and we have companies that will turn a profit at all costs, including rampant destruction of our only home. However, we felt that there was a space within this framework to interpret 'success' more holistically. After all, a company cannot operate in a world where natural resources and ecosystems are degraded or collapsed beyond all measures that can sustain life.

The foundation for our approach is well established within UK company law, where section 172 of the Companies Act 2006 permits directors to 'have regard for' other stakeholders and factors. The environment is listed as a factor that directors should take account of when making strategic decisions. The simplicity of our intervention allocated a specific director role to Nature and Nature's best interests.

We created a non-executive directorship with a mandate to speak on behalf of Nature at the board, using the non-executive role as opposed to an executive one. By using a non-executive role the person or company holding it was very likely to have significant income elsewhere and to feel independent enough to genuinely hold the rest of the board to account. Again there was clear precedent for this with the UK corporate governance code and UK PLCs who are required to appoint non-executives as part of checks and balances of power.

In this intervention we chose to have Nature represented by a corporate body (Lawyers for Nature CIC). We did this in an attempt to remove the human factor of representation. Companies, as legal entities, can already participate on each other's boards as they have legal personality. This is in stark contrast to Nature, that cannot have legal personality or legal standing of any sort. By using a corporate body we were also able to bring in more humans to speak on behalf of Nature as opposed to just one human director.

Finally, we also changed the objects clause of the company to allow them to consider how they would be in service to all life on Earth by incorporating Nature-positive governance. This is a term we felt incorporated the success of the company, but not for that to be achieved at any cost. It allows the directors to effectively turn down opportunities that would make some money for the company in the short term but ultimately over much longer time horizons would be very destructive to the company, its wider community and Nature.

Q. What is the significance of the purpose clause?

The purpose clause in a company's articles of association allows organisations to embed values and principles that extend beyond shareholder profit and measurements such as returns on capital invested. Since about 1985 when the law changed on objects clauses very few companies have exercised this option to include environmental or social commitments explicitly. This resulted in very few businesses having a clear purpose beyond the wider success of the company. It clearly marked a difference between, say, a charity with a clear public benefit and a profit-making entity. There was no such concept as purpose-driven business in the legislation. This is what made NOTB a pioneering movement. The purpose clause legally underpins Nature's role, cementing it within the company's core objectives. This addition is essential because it gives Nature's representative not only a symbolic presence but also a substantive mandate to advocate for Nature-positive actions. The UK's permissive legal structure supports this, allowing organisations to redefine success through the lens of both business and ecological resilience for the longer term.

Q. What is the difference between appointing 'Nature' (represented by guardians) and appointing an individual to speak in the interest of Nature?

The distinction between appointing a 'Nature' representative and merely designating an individual advocate is crucial to the ethos of Rights of Nature. At its heart, Rights of Nature is about ecocentrism – prioritising ecological systems and health over human-centred perspectives (anthropocentrism). In appointing Nature as a board member represented by guardians, NOTB transcends the limitations of traditional environmental advocacy by establishing a legal structure where Nature itself holds a stake. This form of representation theoretically doesn't even necessitate human guardians; instead, any entity or mechanism that can consistently represent Nature's interests could assume this role.

Q. Why did this happen in the UK? And can this happen in other jurisdictions?

The NOTB movement is very successful in the UK because of our fairly permissive legal structure. UK corporate law offers significant flexibility in defining a company's constitution, including the addition of purpose clauses or the appointment of novel board members like Nature. This flexibility allows UK-based companies to adapt their internal governance structures to emerging societal and environmental concerns in ways that are harder to achieve in jurisdictions with more rigid corporate frameworks.

Moreover, the UK's legal system has been widely exported globally, particularly to Commonwealth countries. This shared legal heritage opens the door for implementing similar governance models in jurisdictions with common law systems. Currently, NOTB is being explored and conversations are happening in countries like New Zealand and Canada, where Rights of Nature movements are gathering momentum. Each of these jurisdictions presents unique opportunities and challenges, but the core idea is universally applicable: Nature's presence within corporate governance structures can serve as a transformative force wherever adaptable legal frameworks exist.

Q. Can non-governmental organisations and charities use this model?

In principle, non-governmental organisations and charities can adopt the NOTB model, and Lawyers for Nature is actively working on frameworks that align with the missions of non-profit organisations and their regulatory framework. Although profit isn't ever a driver for these entities, their activities still significantly impact the environment. NOTB could enhance this type of organisation's ecological accountability, aligning their operations more closely with environmental stewardship. For non-governmental organisations focused on conservation or environmental education, Nature's presence on the board can strengthen their mission, embedding ecological considerations more deeply in strategic planning.

Q. Two years in, what are your reflections on where we're at?

Two years since its launch, NOTB has proven both impactful and instructive. Early adopters of the model report a heightened awareness of environmental considerations in their board discussions, influencing decision-making in subtle but profound ways. By giving Nature an official place, companies have found themselves making choices that have much wider inputs and are more considered than before, not simply because of external pressure but due to an internalised commitment to Nature-positive strategy. The presence of a guardian for Nature has changed the dynamics of board discussions, encouraging all present to consider long-term environmental impacts as intrinsic to corporate health. These reflections are shaping the model's evolution, with future iterations enhancing Nature's role based on matters such as the ethical responsibility business has to future generations and the equitable use of resources across longer time horizons.

The legal bit

The following legal breakdown is what's freely shared on Faith In Nature's website. It's a bit like when shampoo ads cut away for 'the science bit' to prove their products really work. Here's 'the legal bit' – the bit that makes this model really work. It was the result of a lot of hand-holding, a lot of very patient explaining, and both parties listening to each other's needs. For the lawyers and the legally literate, this bit's for you. For everyone else, we'll unpack it all in the rest of the book.

The Faith In Nature model

Change 1: Objects clause

We added to our objects clause to allow the company to have specific regard to Nature in our general purpose of promoting the success of the company.

Generally speaking companies' objects are unlimited and contained (post 2006) in the Articles of Association. We wanted to make a statement that would allow us to continue all commercial activities but also demonstrate that we believe we have a longer term purpose which is, in addition to acting to promote the success of the company, that we should have a positive impact on Nature and minimise any harmful impact. We gave constitutional power to the duty to have regard to the environment.

The changes made

We changed the articles of association to include, alongside promoting the success of the company, a long term duty to Nature. This means that we can still progress our business model but we recognise that without a functioning planet, ecosystems and biodiversity we will not be able to continue in the long term. It sets up a purpose that ensures our business decisions are informed and imbued with a long term view of the health of Nature taken as a whole. It also speaks to the concept of holding both Members and Nature as Legal Persons with the right to be named in the objects clause. This is our new wording:

> The objects of the Company are to promote the success of the Company,
>   a. for the benefit of its members; and
>   b. while delivering, through its business and operations, using its best endeavours to
>   i. have a positive impact on Nature as a whole and to
>   ii. minimise the prospect of any harmful impact of the business and operations on Nature,
> in a manner commensurate with the size and resources of the Company, taken as a whole.

The board of directors must act in the way he or she considers, in good faith, most likely to promote the success of the Company in achieving the objects set out above, and in doing so shall have particular regard to impact of the Company's business and operations on the environment and on the affected stakeholders, including Nature and including the likely consequences in the long term.

Nothing in these Articles, whether express or implied, is intended to or shall create or grant any right or any cause of action to, by or for any person other than the Company.

Change 2: Non-Executive Director

We appointed a Non-Executive Director to speak on behalf of Nature. We appointed a corporate director to allow for the rotation and consultation of a number of humans behind the scenes.

The changes made

We appointed Nature as a Non Executive Director on our board of directors and created the ability to delegate the powers to a wider committee. We did this by amending our Articles of Association to entrench the position and used a terms of reference document to outline the duties and responsibilities of the human who acts as the voice of Nature. Nature is currently represented by the not-for-profit legal NGO, Lawyers for Nature. We did this by appointing them as a corporate director at Companies House.

The specific aspects of this arrangement fall under three headings:

1. The NED itself: appointment, entrenchment and removal.
2. Decisions: decision-making processes, voting rights, involvement and delegation of authority.
3. Transparency and accountability.

Each of these can be varied accordingly.

1. The NED

i. We appointed the NED via an ordinary resolution of our shareholders and we changed our articles of association to entrench the position via a special resolution of our shareholders. We used a terms of reference document which includes a consultancy contract for a NED.

ii. To require the board to include the NED in its meetings we included this article:

> **Composition of the Board:** 'The board of directors of the Company from time to time shall include at least one guardian who acts on behalf of Nature.'

We used the following definitions for Nature and Nature Guardian:

- '*Nature* means the natural world and all non-human species that inhabit it and is represented by a director with the requisite expertise and the role to ensure that the board of directors gives due consideration to the environmental impact issues in its decision-making process, for the purpose of achieving the objects of the Company.'
- '*Nature Guardian* means a director acting on behalf of Nature shall be nominated by the Board in accordance with the Nature Nomination Policy and appointed by the holder(s) of a majority of the Voting Shares for the time being in accordance with Article 12.1.'

iii. We entrenched the position by changing our Articles of Association to reference Nature Related Matters and these requiring input from Nature. We also prescribed that the quorum must include Nature where such a declaration had been made. This was the article we inserted:

> **Quorum for directors' meetings**: 'The quorum at any meeting of the directors (including adjourned meetings) shall be 3 directors, provided that, if the agenda of the meeting includes any Nature Reserved Matters, the quorum of such meeting of the directors (including adjourned meetings) shall include Nature.
>
> In respect of any Nature Reserved Matter, the Nature Guardian may provide written materials to be discussed at

the board meetings to be accompanied with the agenda of the meeting.'

iv. We inserted a removal clause as follows:

In the event the Nature Guardian is proposed to be removed from office pursuant to Article 12 or resigns from office, such decision shall be supported with comprehensive and clear reasons, including any information relating to the Nature Guardian's disagreement with the board of the directors.

2. Decisions

i. We gave Nature one vote as a director on our board. The Nature Guardian can also call on a committee of experts to assist with the decision-making.
ii. The Nature Guardian is able to call on and delegate responsibility for decision-making to a committee of experts.

3. Transparency and accountability

i. We inserted a 'provide reasons' clause into our articles to ensure that there was transparency around decisions that concern Nature directly. This is the clause:

Duty to provide reasons when **Board makes decision contrary to the advice of Nature:** 'In the event that the board of directors makes a decision on any Nature Reserved Matters by voting (or otherwise approving, consenting or withholding approval or consent) that is not in the same manner as Nature votes (or otherwise approves, consents or withholds approval or consent), the board of directors shall provide a balanced and comprehensive reasons for such decision. Such decision shall be properly recorded in the form of the resolution in writing or minutes of the meetings of the board of directors as applicable.'

ii. We inserted a clause into our articles of association to ensure there is a reporting obligation once a year on the company. This is the article we used:

> The board of directors shall, for each financial year of the Company, prepare and circulate to its members a Nature Report, the contents of which shall be to the satisfaction of Nature. The Nature Report shall contain a balanced and comprehensive analysis of the impact the Company's business and operations have had, in a manner commensurate with the size and resources of the Company. The Nature Report shall contain such details as necessary to enable the members to have an understanding of the due regard given by the board of directors on the environmental impact issues arising in its decision-making process.

A note on Nature's definition

In the first chapter I mentioned that I consider all beings – humans included – to be part of Nature. But in the legal model here, Nature is defined as the natural world and all *non*-human species that inhabit it.

There is an obvious contradiction here but the choice to exclude humans from the original drafting was deliberate. Until this appointment was made, every director of every company on the planet had either been a human or another company run by humans. Humans already speak in their own best interest so there is a total imbalance of power between humans and all non-human species. We were specifically trying to rebalance this power dynamic by removing the human bias and giving voice to all other beings who, until that point, had been silenced. I wanted a system that encouraged humans to get out of their own way, to be more selfless, and to put the interests of the 'other' first.

If you implement the model and you feel strongly that the definition should include humans then you can, of course, amend it.

3

Gorse: Guardianship and Speaking for Nature

The Common Gorse (Ulex europaeus), also known as Furze or Whin, is the most widespread of seven extremely spiny shrub species found predominantly in the warmer parts of Spain and Portugal but with an obvious Atlantic distribution in Europe. ... The most obvious and striking character of the Ulex species is the dense, very dark-green spines which cover every branch. ... The flowers are a beautiful deep golden yellow, staying in full bloom from July to October. ... The gorse flowers are nectarless but the bees are attracted by the sweet, coconut-scented perfume and by the strong colour which absorbs ultra violet light. (*Gorse*, Humphries and Shaughnessy, 1987)

Guardianship models

The guardianship model was first explained to me by way of comparison with a child needing to appear in court; a child cannot legally represent themselves in a court of law so a responsible adult is required to speak on their behalf. The child, in this case, would be Nature. The responsible adult, the guardian.

Of course, this comparison better explains the mechanics than it does our true relationship with the natural world. Nature isn't silent or incapable of responding to our actions. Nature (in the broadest sense) has simply been shut out of systems designed by humans, exclusively for humans.

Still, the idea itself is elegant and beautiful in its simplicity. But the obvious problem with it comes from an equally simple question: who speaks for Nature?

In Ecuador, any citizen can go to court to defend any aspect of the natural world that they feel is vulnerable. This is probably the truest, most beautiful answer to the question. If somebody feels strongly that they wish to represent a river, or a volcano, or a lily then they are probably well placed to do just that. Generally, the issue is not that there aren't enough people passionate about the natural world who feel compelled to do this, it's that systems don't provide the forum for these people to effect change. But in Ecuador, because the Rights of Nature are recognised at a national level, they have created space for this conversation. Likewise, Nature on the Board (NOTB) creates a similar space.

But what happens if two people have different perspectives on what's best for the river, the volcano or the lily? Worse, what happens if one has ulterior motives? These questions only become more pointed in the business world.

When we realised that every decision a business makes impacts Nature, but the one voice never present was Nature's own, that was recognition that another voice (or voices) needed to join. The aim then must be to bring in another perspective. If business has consistently failed to act in the interests of the natural world, then it is a failure of those too often in power.

Even as boards become more diverse, the roles available stay relatively fixed. The number of people from minority backgrounds on boards may be increasing, but they are still asked to fit the roles of CEO, CFO, COO, and so on. More often than not, this precludes anyone who has not followed a certain educational path, a certain career path or who has not previously worked in a similar organisation – assuming those people even want those roles in the first place.

The guardianship model, on the other hand, allows for a much broader spectrum of perspectives. It allows for the wisdom of First Nations people. It allows for the curiosity of artists. It allows for the idealism of children. Simon Armitage, the UK's poet laureate, said recently in a BBC interview that 'the role of the poet in the contemporary age (is) to speak up for Nature, not just use it in a poem'. Guardianship models allow poets to do just that – in a hands-on, practical way.

Guardianship models can also be used to combine multiple perspectives of what's best for Nature. Whereas I cannot imagine a scenario where multiple people would act together as one CFO, multiple people can (and should) work together as Nature's guardians.

Although rarely verbalised, I sense that the most common pushback to implementing this idea is the perception that it poses some kind of existential threat to the board in its current form. That to invite Nature guardians onto the board is like opening the door to a green police force – an open invitation to shackle the freedoms the board currently enjoys. The opposite is actually true. Nature's guardians are invited onto the board to *help* the board make better, more informed decisions that take the natural world into account. In March 2024, the Commonwealth Climate and Law Initiative, in collaboration with Pollination, arrived at the landmark English law opinion that directors should consider their company's Nature-related risks as part of their duties to promote the success of the company. But if they have so far failed to do so, then how? The answer, surely, must be to have a more open, more inclusive conversation.

So who actually speaks for Nature (now)?

On a few occasions, I've been lucky enough to be guided through rainforests. What would otherwise appear to me a dense, green mass takes on an entirely new form when experienced through the senses of somebody who is at home in that environment. To have such an unfamiliar landscape translated through their senses feels like downloading a software update. They know the calls of the jungle and can mimic the language of the birds; they can explain which plants are cooperating and which are competing; they can show you which plant is a water source and which is a poison; or which plant can heal which ailment and how to prepare it; or which plant has a symbiotic relationship with which animal; or that a certain smell means a certain animal is near; or, or, or …

That is what I hope NOTB can one day do: help us see what is already in plain sight, and help us better understand what we have so far misunderstood. The guides I've met already know what we realised – that it's impossible for any of us to live without making some impact upon the natural world – but they also know how best to manage that impact. They're not superhuman, but actually *human* – still able to use all of their senses in ways most of us never have. And while we all have it in us to operate as they do, they are experts in ways most of us aren't. As with guides, a guardian should help lead the way through unfamiliar territory.

Of course, no one person can speak for all of Nature. It's an impossible ask of one individual and even if one person felt able to speak for the entire natural world, not only would that raise serious red flags, it wouldn't be in Nature's interests to rely upon only one guardian's perspective. It's for these reasons that we created a structure around the role that would both ease the burden on the guardians as well as ensure a diverse and evolving understanding of what's best for Nature. At Faith In Nature, we have the following guidelines:

1. *A shared role*
    Although Nature is one director, two people share the role of Nature's guardians. It is for those guardians to work together to come to a consensus view on what is in Nature's best interests.
2. *The right to consult*
    When dealing with issues that neither guardian feels qualified to advise on, guardians have the right to throw their net wider and consult with whoever necessary. They also have a budget to pay for those expert views if needed.
3. *Short tenure*
    To encourage a diverse and evolving view of Nature's needs, no guardian should be in place for longer than approximately two years.

When we launched NOTB, it was important that our guardians were as credible as the model itself. Ultimately, so much hangs on the people who speak for Nature – both internally, as well as in the eyes of the wider world – that their role carries as much pressure as any other director's. Arguably, it carries even more. (Consider too that India's Ganges and Yamuna rivers were once recognised as legal persons but had that status overturned due to questions over whether their guardians should be liable to pay damages to the families of people who drowned in them. This is not a role without pressure!)

In NOTB's earliest days, it wasn't just Nature's guardians taking a step into the unknown, it was the wider board too – so our guardians needed to speak for Nature as well as guide the board through this period of change. That's why, as our first guardians, we chose Lawyers for Nature and Earth Law Center themselves. They brought a rigour and an integrity to the role which emphasised its ability to cause true systems change. Continuing with the same organisations that had created the model also seemed the best way for everyone else to learn the model's workings, as well as ensuring that the rest of the board stayed on their newly laid rails.

Inevitably, whoever speaks for Nature sets the tone of NOTB. If Nature's guardians are lawyers, NOTB will have a more prominent legal skew. If Nature's guardians are poets, the whole thing will start to feel more poetic. Eventually, NOTB shouldn't feel like one specialism or another, but rather a more holistic perspective. To get to that point, perhaps it's useful to return to the idea of ecological succession.

Every organisation is different and each one is likely to need slightly different things from NOTB. As organisations differ, Nature itself will likely flourish in different ways – exactly as it does in the wild. Likewise, NOTB will be at different stages of development at those organisations where it is implemented. So the question is less 'Who speaks for Nature?' and more 'Who needs to speak for Nature *now*?'

Given this is a move to usher in the Rights of Nature via existing governance models, I think there's a very strong case for the first guardians being Nature lawyers. The movement is still so young, and still so barely understood by most people, that to be in constant conversation with those same lawyers who are designing it is invaluable. They're the people who ensure the system functions and who do so much of the work nobody else notices: establishing the rules, creating legal spaces for the idea to flourish and keeping the board in check so that the whole thing doesn't unravel. Unless an organisation's board is already well versed in those fundamentals, then a grounding in Nature law seems an obvious place to start. Who follows next is less obvious.

So many different people have expressed an interest in becoming Nature guardians. What is heartening is that so many people who hear of this idea want to become part of it. I think *because* it was an idea led by lawyers – because it walks the walk – people who are (rightly) more sceptical of marketing efforts are more open to this. From zoologists to animal whisperers and many in between, each person who puts their hand up for the role of Nature guardian offers the opportunity to shape the future of NOTB, sending it off in one direction or another.

For a Nature guardian to open your eyes to what you couldn't see before, it goes without saying that they should offer expert insight into some aspect of the natural world that you don't already have. This outsider's perspective is what makes it valuable. An outsider perspective not only to your own organisation but, arguably, to boards as a whole. While many people have made a career from serving on boards, the creation of this new role feels like it ought to be filled by people who haven't.

While NOTB does what it says on the tin – brings Nature into the decision-making process at the highest level – its name actually runs the risk of sounding elitist, top-down and, arguably, irrelevant to anyone not already on the board. Obviously, Nature's involvement should be felt throughout the organisation. But whereas many companies are run out of small offices with their manufacturing done by third parties hundreds or thousands of miles away, Faith In Nature manufactures everything itself just outside Manchester. In some ways, a manufacturing company is one of the most operationally complex in which to have launched NOTB. But, because there are fewer third parties, it also offers the opportunity for greatest change – providing everybody feels a *part* of that change.

A focus at Faith In Nature has been ensuring the conversation is as accessible as possible to as many people as possible – both within the company and the surrounding community. The company is also in the process of moving site, so there exists the opportunity to create a space that helps ground this conversation in the everyday. And so, in February 2024, we chose as our next guardian somebody who'd been doing this for over 20 years: Dr Juliet Rose.

Juliet's background is in plant science, horticulture and ecological restoration. She is also Head of Development at the Eden Project where her role includes the development of Nature connection programmes, the National Wildflower Centre and Eden international projects. And so, considering Faith In Nature's product (rooted in the use of plants and herbalism), its new site (and the opportunity to restore industrial land) as well as its internal needs (community engagement), Juliet was ideally placed for the role. (That she is also lovely and a pleasure to work with made it a no-brainer.)

She is also much better placed to speak about ecological succession than me. On asking where she saw herself within this extended metaphor, she answered: 'Personally, I am a big fan of nitrogen fixers like gorse – I see myself as one of those, adding nutrients that will create the conditions for other species to grow and thrive.'

Alongside Juliet, we are working on appointing a hive-mind of guardians – a sub-board, if you like – represented on the board by one spokesperson from that group. This leap is an effort to speed up the process of succession, to bring as many perspectives as possible to the board, in as short a time-frame as possible. Although succession follows an order, it is not entirely linear. There comes a point, when the groundwork has been done, that the conditions are right for many different species to flourish. In guardians' perspectives, as in Nature, (bio)diversity is the ultimate goal.

If all this sound radical, the future might look even more so. Hypothetically, the model allows for any being to serve as Nature guardian. Theoretically, there is nothing that precludes a pig or a snake or a pelican serving as a guardian – other than the obvious problem that none currently could. But that they can't is our doing. We designed this system exclusively for ourselves – so is it fair that in other species' absence, we do as we choose? And how might this change if, somehow, other beings *were* able to participate?

Perhaps, one day, such a line of thinking won't seem so far-fetched. Artificial intelligence (AI) has already decoded our own language(s) and is rapidly advancing our ability to decode the language of other species too. Founded in 2017, the Earth Species Project aims to do precisely this. As they so elegantly put it: 'More than 8 million species share our planet. We only understand the language of one.'

Are other species speaking to each other about the intersection between capitalism and the Rights of Nature? Likely not. But it is fair to assume they communicate their feelings about their worlds to one another. Do they feel safe? Comforted? Threatened? Do they feel joy? Or worry? Or loss?

I write this with 'my' dog, Sonic, curled up beside me. I *know* she feels these things. And I know too *when* she feels these things – because she tells me. We don't have the luxury of developing such a relationship with whales, or orangutans or polar bears. But a whale is better placed than many of us to speak to the health of the oceans, an orangutan of the forests and a polar bear of the Arctic. If AI really can help bridge the gap between species, then to continue to ignore the voices of other species will be an act of wilful negligence.

Perhaps more immediately achievable, though perhaps more radical still, might be the development of an AI guardian that could assess what is best for Nature as a whole. If this were possible, it could further reduce human bias – while still being able to understand the human-made constructs of boards, businesses and even the Rights of Nature. This would be true ecocentric thinking. What then might it consider to be in the best interests of Nature, as a whole? And does the idea fill you with hope? Or dread? If it conjures nightmarish images, I would argue they can't be more nightmarish than what is already happening to us, as the ecosystem upon which all life depends falls apart. Personally, I'd want to hear this other perspective. At its heart, NOTB is an admission that we need help. If a guardian can offer a helpful perspective, then it ought to be heard – whether from a human or otherwise.

For those who disagree, the good news is that – fascinating as this line of thinking may be – such speculation has little impact on how NOTB operates in the here and now. The time-frames for such advances are unknown and a bridge to be crossed when, and if, we come to it. For now, I'm more worried about what state the natural world will be in by the time we reach that bridge, if we ever do.

Perhaps the tools we already have – our humanity, our empathy and our imaginations – are the tools we really need to master to make the changes necessary.

What would Nature say?

Through listening to our guardians speak, my entire understanding of subjects has changed – not least my understanding of governance and the law, whether that be Nature law or even corporate law itself. Great companies are run by great boards performing their duties really, really well. They mitigate shareholders' risks – because that is what boards are currently *for*. But Nature is also, obviously, at risk. And Nature is also, obviously, a major stakeholder. With this perspective shift, the entire role of a board can be re-evaluated, and there's no better way to do this than with Nature actually in the room.

This was never about pitting the interests of shareholders against Nature's interests, but recognising that we must *also* acknowledge Nature as another significant stakeholder. When we do that, boards' focus will naturally begin to shift – because that will *become* what they are for. No longer will we be weighing the impact of our decisions with one hand, but with both.

But other, more everyday, conversations also take a different turn – like that of the supply chain which, at Faith In Nature, is a forever conversation. It will never end because our options never end. As a company reliant on plants, we need to understand how their world is changing. We can't afford to become over-reliant on any one plant given the very real risk that any number of the plants we use may become unavailable at short notice. In which case, we need to understand which other plants have the same properties; which are available now and which might be available in the future; which might be more accessible (and what that might mean for cost); which might thrive when others suffer; how certain plants are grown and how *where* they're grown impacts biodiversity; and which of the never-ending developments might change everything.

And, of course, we also need to understand what *they* need from us. How should we change our behaviour? What should we give back? How can we help them thrive? This is not entirely altruistic, but nor is it wholly selfish. It's simply recognising the interconnectedness of all things – and so this becomes a circular conversation of a reciprocal relationship.

Prior to first launching NOTB, many people may have asked why we'd want a conservationist (or a zoologist or a botanist or, or, or ...) serving on a company board. I've seen enough to know the more pertinent question is: *Why wouldn't we?!* It seems almost unthinkable now that we wouldn't want a plant scientist's perspective – because it is clearly in Nature's interests for us to have this deeper knowledge, and *also* in the shareholders' interests too.

But there is also a simpler, more everyday aspect to encouraging a mindset of Nature-first enquiry. Sometimes Faith In Nature relies on the heavy lifting of NOTB, but often a much more grounded question is all that's needed: *What would Nature say?* It's actually so simple, we wrote a song about it. Its first verse goes:

> *If you're wondering what to do*
> *Take a walk outside, it might give you a clue.*
> *A little thought goes a long, long way, but...*
> *You probably already know.*
> *Hey, what would Nature say?*

It might sound silly, but if we ask ourselves that question – What would Nature say? – and encourage its use in our everyday undertakings, we might find that for many of our simpler conundrums, we already know the answer. It's not that we don't know right from wrong, or that we don't know what's actually best for Nature, it's that we just aren't asking the right questions. Or, if we are, we're not being given the opportunity to do anything about it.

That question is now everywhere at Faith In Nature. Everyone has permission to ask it, answer it and act upon it. We've even had it thrown back at us on the factory floor. This is great! Through nurturing this approach, everyone can take a step into a guardian's role. And what we begin to see happening is that the question is being asked independently, earlier and earlier in the decision-making process, long before it even enters the boardroom. The upshot is that, in most cases, the best Nature-positive decisions have been made before Nature even has to input.

Already, some of Faith In Nature's most interesting supply chain developments are coming from people elsewhere in the business because NOTB gives them a clearer understanding of what it is the board wants. And those changes are already on shelves. In July 2024, Faith In Nature relaunched every one of its products – with Nature a director throughout the entire development process.

On being a guardian

There are tensions at play in being a guardian. One such tension is that on the one hand, a guardian is asked to speak not as themselves, but in the interests of the wider natural world. On the other hand, guardians are chosen for their particular specialism. Another tension is that there is a degree of role-play involved in acting as a guardian – a shedding of one's own skin. However, speaking as Nature is perhaps a truer reflection of our true natures than many of the other titles we give ourselves.

Quite how a guardian keeps themselves grounded and connected to the needs and wants of the natural world is personal to them. Likewise, how a guardian weighs up whether a decision is truly in the interest of the natural world is a matter for their judgement. As yet, there is no set protocol for making such decisions, but useful filters exist, such as the practice of asking whether an action is Respectful, Regenerative and Reciprocal.

But while much of the guardian's role is to be refined by the guardian themselves, there are many things the company can do to make the role more manageable. These stem from taking time to consider what rights are already granted to other (human) employees, and taking time to grant those same rights to Nature (as a director).

If Nature (as a director) is equal to all other directors, then Nature ought to share the same rights other directors likely take for granted. Nature's substantive rights are the ones that grab the headlines: Nature has the right to be named as a stakeholder, Nature has the right to be heard and Nature has the right to a vote. Ultimately, all these should result in Nature's right to thrive. But for those rights to be enforced, Nature also needs procedural rights in the day-to-day running of the company.

Those procedural rights might include: the right to access information (in order to make decisions), the right to time (to research the appropriate responses), the right to consult (with other experts), the right to a budget (to spend however Nature deems necessary), the right to make its own judgements (of how to do its job) and, of course, the right to direct the actions of the company.

In terms of time commitments, guardians each spend around two days in the business per month. Because there are at least two of them, and they might choose to split their time, this means that their presence is always felt.

At Faith In Nature, the board is not quorate for a 'Nature Related Matter' unless Nature is present, so at least one of Nature's guardians is present at all board meetings. To ensure Nature's presence is not only confined to board meetings, further Nature Related Matters meetings occur once a fortnight in which the agenda is Nature's to dictate. This is the forum for other directors to bring to Nature's attention any issues they feel are relevant and for Nature to ask questions of its own.

Ultimately, the role of guardian is not formulaic. Nor should it ever be. As rewilders of the boardroom, the last thing we want is for Nature's guardians to become business robots. If a board is operating outside its comfort zone by inviting Nature into the conversation, it's worth remembering that a guardian is also likely out their comfort zone. That too is one of the tensions. They chose a Nature-based path over one in business management – and that's precisely why we need them.

The right to reply

Included within the NOTB framework is a request to the board that they report back to Nature at the end of each year. That report should contain an overview of all processes, conversations and decisions resulting from NOTB in that year. Those reports are public and verified by Nature's guardians as being an accurate reflection of events.

These reports exist primarily as a safeguard against greenwashing. Only through transparency and openness can the initiative become self-policing. If a company claims to have appointed Nature to their board but doesn't publish an annual report – verified by their Nature guardians – it's worth asking why. At least with everything in the open, the public are better placed to question whether or not that company is really embracing the spirit of NOTB.

One of Nature's procedural rights is the right to reply. The last section of the annual report is given to Nature's guardians, where they are free to share their thoughts without editing or interference from the company. In that spirit, it seems right to give the rest of this chapter to Juliet.

The UK countryside is so green that it's easy to forget that it is one of the most Nature-depleted countries in the world. The picture isn't any better elsewhere, as other countries seem to be following our example, and species continue to go extinct. The world's weather systems are increasingly unstable, veering from drought to flood, while deforestation and resource depletion continue – all of this puts further pressure on Nature. Despite these visible threats to Nature, this crisis is also a Nature-funding crisis.

I find it astonishing that investing in Nature is often viewed as risky, expensive, complex and messy – all terms I would associate with *not* doing something about climate change and biodiversity loss. It seems certain we will be wrangling with a future that will be all these things if we don't look after the best system we have for dealing with climate change – Nature. Nothing comes close to the power of Nature in managing carbon, regulating water and cooling the planet.

Yet there is a global shortfall in biodiversity funding running at hundreds of billions of dollars every year. The big question is where the money will come from – not only to put things right but to help Nature thrive. At the moment, most of the money to support global biodiversity comes from governments (along with a very small amount from global philanthropy, which, in general, supports many more social causes than environmental ones). The Nature-funding crisis is complex, though. It's not just about mobilising money for Nature restoration and conservation, though these things are really important. As well as reconsidering current investment, it's also about encouraging more investment in other things that can support Nature, like regenerative agriculture and biotechnology. This means there is a vital role for business. That role means fully recognising the natural resources the business uses on its balance sheet and making investments in Nature that can help us reverse the situation we are in.

A Nature-positive business has to go beyond its supply chains and reflect its consideration of Nature in its culture, leadership, values and purpose. A Nature guardian can help encourage and reveal the many skills, experiences and assets that already exist within a business that could be used to deliver more Nature-positive action. That could be considering the company's estate, or how it can encourage more Nature connection for its staff and customers or providing advocacy and increasing awareness for Nature using its communication skills and channels. In a crisis, everything counts – whether it's working with like-minded suppliers, developing new types of products, addressing water, energy and waste, creating space for Nature within the footprint of premises, encouraging clients to support the Nature and climate bill, or making direct investments in Nature conservation and restoration. There are many ways in which businesses can change their relationship with Nature for the better.

As for how it feels to actually represent Nature (all living things everywhere!) on a board ... actually, it feels great! Even cathartic – in the way that fighting someone's corner does. Yes, there is the overwhelming impossibility of being able to represent something so vast, but this is about giving a voice to something that, despite its huge relevance, isn't invited or even often heard in the boardroom. This can bring a huge sense of purpose for those who choose to represent Nature.

Around the world, different models are being explored to influence Nature-positive decisions in the boardroom, such as better training for board members, committing to environmental standards or accreditation, or consulting with external experts. However, the impact of actually having someone in the role and room for whom representing Nature is their core purpose should not be underestimated. A Nature guardian is a voting member of the board – not an advisor. It is a leadership role that has the weight to influence decisions. Its role is as much to ask awkward but informed questions as to answer them. For despite appearances, many businesses still only pay lip service to supporting Nature, and because they often operate at a distance from long and complex supply chains, few are aware of their full impact on the natural world. But Nature guardians must also listen to concerns, not simply state their demands, and they should give affirmation for good ideas. In essence, Nature guardians are there to continually remind us that we are all part of Nature. They should help guide decision-making in a way that is Nature-positive and, therefore, people-positive and ultimately profit-positive.

NOTB is a way to encourage companies to think beyond their immediate performance. The Nature guardians' role might be to encourage boards not to rush but instead invest in the time and expertise to enable better long-term decision-making. Some Nature guardians may bring their own networks that can better connect the business to Nature-related risk or opportunity. The role could also be to provide endorsement for decisions that will likely lead to more Nature-positive outcomes, such as Nature-positive innovations and products. A Nature guardian could also operate beyond the confines of the board, for example, encouraging greater staff inclusion by providing a conduit for Nature-related ideas or problems to be received and considered at board level from across the business, especially people involved in day-to-day processes. Nature guardians may have a creative role in helping to shape advocacy or communication campaigns that can speak for Nature and help give visibility to the demonstration of Nature-positive actions that deserve it. Encouraging a company culture and influencing a company's purpose might actually be an integral part of the role. Incorporating Nature into a company's thinking and policies isn't a short-term project you can complete and sign off; it's an ongoing essential part of any business that will need to be continually addressed.

Ultimately, it's my belief that NOTB should create an organisational culture that ensures all employees are aware of how Nature relates to their jobs, where each member of staff is supported and given license to use their own creativity to find a better way of doing business, and that recognises the rights of and reliance on Nature.

What is interesting about NOTB is how far the concept could go. Although the concept started in the corporate sector (where it continues to gain traction), it has the capacity to operate in all sectors of our society; indeed, this is already starting to happen as we see voluntary sector organisations, large and small, start to embrace the idea too. We live within a closed system on this planet – every decision made affects planetary resources – which means there is a need for Nature to be represented throughout. Imagine Nature being represented at a local level on parish councils and neighbourhood planning groups, in schools and community groups. What if we start to think of NOTB at a national level? Could the new Nature and Climate Envoys occupy a similar role in government?

However NOTB develops, it is not a 'nice to have'. Increasingly, companies will have to respond to Nature-related regulations, legal duties and disclosure of risks. Having access to Nature-related expertise at board level could become a core requirement – especially as board members will become more accountable for non-compliance with sustainability disclosures as well as potential liability for greenwashing.

For too long, we have failed to recognise that other species have a right to thrive on this planet. We need to accept that their success and ours are inextricably linked. Perhaps we should hang a banner in every board room that says, 'Please remember when making decisions today that without Nature, you could not exist; you aren't the only species living on this planet, and future generations would also like to live here too.'

4

Willow: Nature on the Board, Out in the Wild

Long before the advent of mankind, the Willow (genus Salix) thrived throughout the world. Plants belonging to this genus are amongst the earliest recorded pre-Ice Age flowering plants. ... It is easy to understand that Salix, being one of the earliest colonizers of glacial sediment, thrived and spread over considerable distances during this period. Seed dispersal has always played a significant part in the distribution of Salix species, their seeds being extremely small and tufted, with fine hairs encouraging wind dispersal over wide areas. ... Today, Salix species are present in almost every part of the world. ... They are most numerous throughout the British Isles, Europe, Asia, Japan, China, North America and Canada. They also exist as dwarf species in the Arctic. (*Willows: The Genus Salix*, Newsholme, 2022)

How might business change if Nature had a voice and a vote?

When we launched Nature on the Board (NOTB) out into the wild – open-sourcing the framework for others to implement too – we had no idea how many other companies might follow, how quickly, or what type of company they might be. But we knew we didn't want this to stop with us.

Would we be inundated? Or would it be tumbleweeds? It became immediately apparent that the levels of interest were way beyond what we'd dared imagine. Come summer 2023, the story had reached hundreds of millions of people. By that time, we'd done the speaking rounds and answered as many requests for information as we could. And we'd spoken to all kinds of companies – not just the obvious 'good' ones. We spoke to suppliers of Fast Moving Consumer Goods (FMCGs), banks, funds, insurers, real estate developers, IT firms, outdoor companies, architects, travel agents, media companies, film production companies, machine rental firms … even zoos. Our pitch was the same to all of them: we'll only really figure out how this works when it's not just us doing it. In almost all cases, I got the sense that they genuinely wanted to – but, for whatever reason, didn't. In sales terms, we had more leads than we knew what to do with, but couldn't close the deal.

Then in August 2023 came the news that Nature had joined the board of Friends of Cave Creek Canyon (FOCCC), a non-profit volunteer organisation that exists to inspire appreciation and understanding of the beauty, biodiversity and legacy of Cave Creek Canyon in south-east Arizona. Despite all the companies interested, it wasn't another company that jumped with us, but a group of volunteers in a desert 8,000 miles away. And then came news that another company had. And then another. And another. And … to quote Paulo Coelho: 'Everything that happens once can never happen again. But everything that happens twice will surely happen a third time.'

Every organisation mentioned in this chapter is extraordinary. They've all chosen to walk the walk, to take a leap into the unknown, to be part of trying to find a solution. I've only included those with whom I've had direct, meaningful contact – but I know this list is growing and will undoubtedly have changed between the time of writing and the time of publication.

To have been first to implement the NOTB method was a privilege. To many, I'm sure it also marked us out as weird, or eccentric, or theatrical. But to see others adopt it too is an even greater privilege. It's all the others that make the weird normal. And, in a way, that's even more important.

Friends of Cave Creek Canyon

Other than now both having Nature on our boards, a soap company in Manchester doesn't seem to share much in common with a volunteer group in Portal, Arizona. But that's precisely why I was so delighted when Rene Donaldson of FOCCC told me they'd appointed Nature to their board – because it showed NOTB is an idea that doesn't fit neatly into just one box. It's an idea that resonates there as much as it does here – because the challenges we both face are the same. Wherever we are, whatever we do, the threat *Nature* faces is the same.

I'd met Rene some years earlier in Osa, Costa Rica. She and her husband, Tony, were standing on the same platform as Anne and I – captivated by the jungle before us. Rene was dressed just as colourfully as the birds she was watching, and Tony was wielding a camera with a lens longer than a Resplendent Quetzal's tail feather. Some people, I'm sure, you're just meant to meet. After we each went our separate ways, we stayed in touch – as they opened up their incredible world to us and we did to them. They are, simply, wonderful.

So when I first wrote to her telling her about NOTB, it wasn't a sales pitch. It was just me sharing news of what we'd been doing. I didn't expect that between emails, Rene would have read extensively on the Rights of Nature, altered the mechanics of the model to suit a charitable organisation and tabled the motion that FOCCC should appoint Nature to their board. I just love the hands-on, no-fuss spirit with which this idea was received, adapted and put into action.

'We thought it might be a means to involve younger people in Friends of Cave Creek Canyon since the forest is their legacy,' said Rene.

The proposal hatched with three proxies who will speak for Nature yet Nature only has one vote like other board members. I would have preferred to give Nature veto power, but I knew if I included it in the proposal that the motion would not pass. No other board member holds that power. The proxies decide among themselves who will attend a board meeting, and proxy names are not announced publicly. Nature alone is the board member. Three proxy positions are required in order to ensure one in attendance at every monthly meeting, especially since younger people work or attend classes. Finding the candidates for the proxy positions was difficult. Portal, Arizona, located in the Chiricahua Mountains, is 60 miles from the nearest store with no cell-phone reception in the canyon. With effort, however, two of the three proxy positions were filled with interested, younger people. The third proxy position was filled by a retiree who is most excited to speak on Nature's behalf. We discussed as a board that this will be an experiment, and we will work through problems as they arise.

FOCCC operates the Cave Creek Canyon Visitor Information Center in the Coronado National Forest as well as managing Willow Tank, the only reliable source of water for birds and animals on the east side of the Chiricahua Mountains. Situated at the convergence of four ecozones – the Sonoran and Chihuahuan deserts, the Rocky Mountains and Sierra Madre Occidental – the Chiricahua Mountains constitute the largest biodiverse land area in North America with half of North American birds and bats, more than three-quarters of the lizards, and a large proportion of the ants. And it's at Willow Tank where Rene describes a tangible example of NOTB in action:

Cattails (Typha latifolia) have overrun Willow Tank with heavy rainfall last fall. Our president introduced the idea to import muskrats, native to Arizona. They occupy marshes, streams, ponds, and lakes with fresh and brackish water. They live in dens with tunnels built into riverbanks. They also eat cattails which is why the idea appealed. After this board meeting, Nature got on the stick and researched the problem, deciding that the rodents would undermine the integrity of the tank sides by burrowing into them for dry den sites. At the next meeting, Nature reported the research and the board immediately dropped the idea which never made it to a motion.

It's simple, isn't it? That last line really sticks with me: *Nature reported the research and the board immediately dropped the idea.* So much about this idea is self-evident. When we change our structures to make space for a Nature-first perspective, then allow that perspective to be brought forward and listened to, decisions are often a no-brainer.

Sometimes such decisions can feel underwhelming, lacking drama or a Hollywood ending. Here, the decision to leave well alone is to change nothing. It doesn't seem particularly noteworthy – but it might prove to be for those at Willow Tank who rely upon it. Imagine how different the world might be today if, decades ago, we'd all collectively adopted a NOTB approach to decision-making. If we'd all left alone what wasn't ours to interfere with. At its simplest and humblest, NOTB is just an invitation to slow down and think twice about our impact upon all beings who also call this planet home.

For me, this example alone makes NOTB a success. That the framework led to the safeguarding of a watering hole relied upon by so much life is precisely why it exists. This idea is not about the idea itself, nor the organisations that implement it, but about *Nature* – however far beyond our daily lives the changes occur.

With thanks to FOCCC, and especially to Rene, this chapter celebrates willow. In terms of succession, willow represents a step on from pioneer plants. Willow is an intermediate species – a bridge from the early successional species that often go unnoticed to the later climax species that represent a transformed landscape.

House of Hackney

The longer I spend with this idea, the more I wonder if the most important movers are not those who move first, but those who move second, third, fourth … ten thousandth.

In moving first, the sceptic can always argue that we did it for the publicity. As an advertising creative, I'm not naïve – of course we knew it would generate headlines, and we've made a name for ourselves in corners of the world where our products might never even sell. But those who follow aren't guaranteed that level of exposure, and still they do it anyway. They are the ones that turn a story into a movement – and by adding their numbers, the movement gathers strength. Today, Nature has a voice and a vote in a handful of boardrooms, but if Nature is to gain a foothold in the way companies are run, then that will be down to 'the normalisers'.

They're everyone else who stood up beside Spartacus and shouted 'I am Spartacus!' Without them, Spartacus would have died. They're the real heroes of that scene.

Of all the companies that lent their support to NOTB, none did more than House of Hackney – a British interiors, fashion and lifestyle company founded by Frieda Gormley and Javvy M. Royle. From first meeting with them, their enthusiasm was infectious. Their love of the natural world resonated as deep and true. They'd always seen Nature as a muse and set up their company as a way of bringing Nature into their home. Though operating in a different space to Faith In Nature, there is something of a shared spirit between the companies. I sensed they wanted to shake things up just as much as we did and, when I asked them why they took the step that so many others only talked about taking, I saw that there were far more similarities than I'd first realised. As Frieda so beautifully put it:

> Over time, as we observed Nature's prints and palettes through the design process, Nature started to become our teacher. We started looking at Nature's

living systems and circadian rhythms, its ebbs and flows and we wondered how can we could bring this into our organisation? Nature was already giving us so much inspiration, wisdom and, obviously, economic services ... there was very much this rising consciousness that there's so much to learn from Nature. In 2022, when Patagonia made Mother Earth its only shareholder, then you gave Mother Nature a seat at the table, that really blew our minds. We just realised that this is what we must do.

I see in this the exact same creative process we went through, albeit with different names. House of Hackney saw Mother Nature as their muse. We saw Nature as our Creative Director. We were both looking for ways to model our businesses on natural systems that are already perfect. There is also that sense of inevitability about the move that we first felt. If you feel as we do about this, when you realise it's possible, it's not something you can turn down.

Javvy also points to something we felt:

When you talk about climate, you can point to a cloud. But when you mention the word Nature, everyone has an immediate connection to it. Everyone can do this. Everyone lives within Nature's systems. They just need to open up their eyes to what they're doing and why they're doing it.

I sense within them what I feel in myself: a need to tell a different story. Not a 'sustainability' story, but the oldest story known to humankind: that of the world around us.

And in October 2023, again with the help of Lawyers for Nature, they appointed not only (Mother) Nature to their board, but Future Generations too. The two, of course, go hand in hand. If we manage to protect something of the natural world, the benefits might be felt most by those who come later. And that doesn't just mean future generations of humans, but future generations of all beings. Sometimes I hear the pushback that it is us who are in danger, not Nature – that Nature will carry on with or without us. In the most detached sense possible, that might be true. But it is *this* version of Nature I feel connected to. It is these beings alive today who also have the right to a future and who rely upon us to protect their future generations.

That House of Hackney took the same basic model and twisted it to recognise this nuance is brilliant. As with FOCCC, they too saw it for what it is: a model that can be made to work for whatever organisation is willing to make it work. That is despite them facing challenges we didn't.

Faith In Nature is still independent and family owned, meaning we are afforded a great deal of freedom. But, like many companies, House of Hackney already had investors who took a little more persuading. It took compromise and not losing sight of the bigger picture. Done really is better than perfect, so the priority was to get it over the line then tighten it later. 'At the end of the day', said Javvy, 'everyone still wants to do good and be good. It's human nature, so I don't think it was a tall ask. It was just them getting their heads round it'.

Whereas many might worry that the model isn't yet perfect, or their business isn't yet perfect (which is obviously true of all businesses!), House of Hackney are willing to figure things out as they go. They're willing to ask the difficult questions and curious to find better answers. From working to find the true cost of their supply chain, to planning a regenerative future supply of wood for their wallpaper, to saying no to certain partnerships in faith that the right ones will replace them – what speaks to me most of all about their approach is their comfort in this uncertain space. That, to me, is the creative process. It is also the founder spirit speaking.

They are a lesson in just getting on and doing it – because Mother Nature and future generations are relying on us to do things differently.

Start and end of life

Following House of Hackney, the next company to announce their appointment of Nature to their board was Intradrive – a small start-up manufacturing e-bike components. Again, on the face of it, there is little to connect a soap company, an interiors company and an e-bike company. But to know that Nature's voice

52

is beginning to be heard across different industries, at different scales – and not only at companies with 'Nature' in their name or visual identity – is a sign that things are changing.

It is also interesting to note that this move was driven by Intradrive's investor who clearly recognises there is more than one type of return on investment. One type of return is financial. Another is a shift towards a system that better protects the natural world. Most likely, progressive investors want both – but if an investor is willing to accept either one or the other, then they can't lose.

There is also the question of timing. Generally, more established companies have more stakeholders. More stakeholders mean more opinions – and, invariably, some will resist inviting Nature's voice into proceedings. Still, it represents a great opportunity for start-ups and their backers to grow the Nature-positive businesses of the future. To start a company is already a risk – and entrepreneurs might be more comfortable with this than the investors who might come later. In 2022, 91 per cent of UK companies had less than a £1 million turnover. In 2023, 900,000 new businesses were formed. Of course, not all have boards and not all have investors. But for those that have both, there is huge opportunity for the small businesses and their backers to take great strides forward.

Gower Street (formerly the Marple Charitable Trust) is a foundation set up by Sophie and Nick Marple to fund education work in the UK and Ghana. In 2018, they pivoted the majority of their funds to address the climate crisis and, given the urgency, committed to a total spend-down by 2028. At the time of writing, Nature is about to be named director.

Theirs is an eye-opening example with profound implications. It is one thing to recognise the Rights of Nature and grant Nature the power to defend itself, but how does Nature actually pay for that legal protection? The lawyers I've met in this space are, of course, driven by more than money – but they still need to eat and earn a living. If Nature doesn't have a bank account, how can it pay for the protection it needs? And when lawyers choose their practice area, wouldn't it be wonderful for them not to have to choose between protecting Nature and protecting those who destroy Nature but pay more? Could Gower Street's appointment of Nature to its board be the first example of Nature being given genuine hold of the purse strings? Could it be Nature's first bank account?

And what does it suggest about those organisations not at the start of their lives, but at their ends? Gower Street have a clear end in sight. Come 2028, their time will be up and their money will be spent. Start-ups are so often touted as the great agitators, but could it actually be those at the end of their lifecycles that have an even greater appetite for risk? For shaking things up as they leave. For ensuring they're remembered as what Roman Krznaric terms 'good ancestors'?

In any case, it is inevitable that plenty of business – and likely whole industries – will continue to close. In 2022, the Office for National Statistics reported that more businesses closed in the UK than opened. Many will have closed through no choice of their own – but it's unlikely any business will be around forever, and many have already outstayed their welcome. For those that ought to be hospiced, they should also consider how they'll clean up on their way out.

The term 'de-growth' carries with it all kinds of baggage, but many business people I've met are comfortable speaking about deceleration: accepting that slower rates of growth – or, simply, reaching 'maturity' – is healthy and more sustainable. Charities too ought to plan for their eventual demise – not with dread, but with hope that they no longer need to exist.

Gower Street may be Nature's case study on how to exit with grace.

Acting locally

If Manchester is home of the Industrial Revolution – which may have brought great economic benefits but has also had a devastating impact on Nature – then it's strangely fitting that Nature is regaining its voice in the same city some 200 years later. At the time of writing, in addition to Faith In Nature's Manchester-based board, NOTB has also been implemented by two other nearby organisations.

The Better Business Network – a network of purpose-driven companies – opened their 2024 summit by announcing that they

too had appointed Nature to their board. Their appointment was marked by an immediate and visible difference: a Nature guardian present on every one of the summit's panels – some of whom wore golden stag's heads, capes of beach plastic or had their mouths gaffer-taped shut. Offering their insights, and contrasting those with the other panellists, it brought real theatre to the idea. (Who said governance can't also be fun?) And it also meant that every business present – gathered from across the UK – left with a much greater awareness of NOTB. Given the environmental impact of the events industry in general, it's a brave move to have tackled this head-on and I hope other sustainability events follow this lead.

In July 2024, Future Everything – an arts organisation that exists at the convergence of art, technology and society – announced that they too would be appointing Nature to their board. Currently still in the development stage, their challenge is to imagine how this works for a non-profit organisation and how the arts can help deepen our understanding of what it really means to make space for Nature. In developing their model, they have drawn together a working group of writers, philosophers, artists, lawyers and First Nations peoples – again proving the importance of creativity in reimagining the status quo.

But this is not about Manchester, or really anywhere in particular, but more so the idea that NOTB may take hold when communities feel passionate about *their* Nature. We may lack a frame of reference for Nature more broadly, but most of us have connections to local landscapes that we call home.

Might pride in local areas, or love of our land, accelerate the adoption of NOTB more broadly? I have already met with people interested in appointing Nature to their town's council. Likewise, I've met with real estate developers, construction companies, sports clubs, schools, theatres, museums and national parks. In one town hall, the idea was floated that every business in the town appoint Nature to their boards. Imagine!

These are the spaces that create communities. The Rights of Nature needn't remain an abstract concept if Nature can be given a seat at the tables of all the smaller, localised groups who form the basis of our everyday lives.

A small, contained vision of this future might also be emerging on Rathlin Island – Northern Ireland's only inhabited island. Funded by the Arts and Humanities Research Council, 'Future Island-Island' is an ongoing project working with the island's 141 inhabitants to find design-led answers for the green transition, spanning many aspects of community life: economy, culture, education, tourism, ecology and civic engagement. Nature has already been given a seat on Rathlin's civic assembly – which is, in effect, a small 'board' or group of citizens selected to represent the views of the wider community. Other members of that assembly were chosen at random, but the one seat pre-selected was Nature's. For an island community like Rathlin's, Nature's role in their everyday lives is impossible to ignore. Those who live closest to the elements will feel Nature's impact even more acutely. By the same measure, they'll know better than most how humanity's actions impact upon the natural world. In this sense, perhaps communities like Rathlin's have long treated Nature as a significant stakeholder. Perhaps NOTB just gives a name to what they were already doing. Regardless, that they should recognise it and make it official is a seismic shift for the dynamics of a small community and is eminently replicable for all willing community groups.

When we act locally, involving all members of the community and encouraging everyone to take ownership of an idea like NOTB, we are no longer acting *as if* Nature has rights. When we come together and agree to tell a different story, Nature *does* have rights. And, together, we get to demonstrate what that looks like. Whether our communities are companies or islands, if Nature can be recognised as a stakeholder within them *and* those communities can flourish, it holds a mirror up to the wider world and asks if it can be made to work in one place, then why not all places?

Flowing from the Whanganui to the Usk

The Whanganui has played such an important part in this story. It inspired us, helped us realise what might be possible, and is mentioned time and again by people I speak to about this work. Perhaps only a river could carve through the rock of our thinking the way the Whanganui has. But magnificent as I'm sure the Whanganui is, I haven't ever visited. I haven't even been to New Zealand. But I have wandered the rivers I know, closer to home, wondering how we might protect these waters too. If one river is sacred, so are all rivers. If one river should have its rights recognised, so should all rivers. And why stop at rivers? Likewise, so should all tributaries. So should their ultimate destination: the sea. So should all land. All beings. But, sticking with rivers for the time being …

In the UK, we cannot legally recognise rivers as legal people in the same way they were able to with the Whanganui. But NOTB seems to offer some hope here too. By strange quirk of fate, many UK rivers also have boards. Or, more specifically, there are 'Nutrient Management Boards' – groups of stakeholders (water companies, farmers, ecologists, and so on) – tasked with managing the nutrient levels in the rivers. Realising, perhaps, that this was weirdly specific and didn't allow for a fuller, more holistic view, some of these have recently been replaced by Catchment Partnerships, which aim to deliver improvements across key issues on water quality, wildlife and sustainable land use. And it is via this series of loopholes that the Usk's Catchment Partnership has been able to use a version of NOTB to appoint Nature (the river Usk) to its own board.

It's a messier, more convoluted approach to recognising a river's rights – but it intends towards the same outcome. And to all intents and purposes, it looks much the same. In both cases, a guardian of that river speaks for that river and it's fitting that a river should take the path of least resistance in ushering in the Rights of Nature through existing frameworks.

The Usk runs through Bannau Brycheiniog (Brecon Beacons) National Park – almost right back at the doorstep of where I call home. On a personal level, it's almost impossible to comprehend that this should have come full circle. But in such a complicated world, such a simple idea cuts through. And it's an idea that can unite us. I was asked to attend the Usk's meeting in which the motion was tabled to implement NOTB. Approximately 20 stakeholders were present, many with strong opinions. After about an hour of discussing NOTB, a hand went up, and a voice said: 'I don't know why we have to talk about it so much when we can just get on and do it.' It was a farmer. We can be quick to point the finger at this group or that group and deflect blame – and, as land owners, farmers are often on the receiving end. As I drive around my local area, I pass signs on one side of the road that read 'No Farmers, No Food' and signs on the other side that read 'No Plants, No Planet'. Both are true – and I sense both viewpoints were in the room that day. But, after a show of hands, the motion was passed. The Usk was given a voice.

Already, I know that the Usk's neighbouring river, the Wye, is to do the same. And if those two rivers can, then why not all rivers? On speaking to Helen Lucocq, who together with Tom Johnstone steered the Usk's appointment of the river to its board, she shared with me a vision of how every tributary be given its own guardian. I think this is such a beautiful idea – to imagine that even the smallest of streams might be given voice by somebody who cares for it, feels protective of it and feels compelled enough to speak for it.

Building resilience to flooding in Wales by 2050

'Building resilience to flooding in Wales by 2050' is the title of a report presented by the National Infrastructure Commission for Wales to the Welsh government in October 2024. It's a thoughtful and thought-provoking piece on how Wales – a small country with 33 rivers, a 1,680-mile coastline and more than its fair share of rainfall – can better prepare for floods that are increasing in regularity and severity. The report makes 17 recommendations. One of them reads: 'Nature as a Stakeholder: By 2028, set up the mechanisms to incorporate nature as a key stakeholder within flooding.'

NOTB was included in the report as a case study of how this might be possible and, at the report's launch event, the feeling in the room echoed that at the Usk's catchment partnership. A sense of 'let's get on with it, already'. How, or if, Welsh government departments implement the model remains to be seen, but Wales already has form for recognising 'invisible stakeholders'. The Well-being of Future Generations Act came into force in Wales in 2016, bringing the needs of our descendants into our decision making today and aiming to ensure that future generations enjoy at least the same quality of life we do now.

Residents of Fairbourne in mid Wales have been told that in 30 years' time, theirs might be the first Welsh village to be underwater. Given the urgency of the situation, it seems right that all proposals are considered. Given the timelines, whether or not NOTB proves to be in any way helpful remains to be seen – but recognising Nature as a stakeholder must be more helpful than pretending otherwise.

Since that report was published, the commission responsible for publishing it have themselves appointed a new commissioner with specific regard for the natural world. The commission's chair, David Clubb, says of the move:

> At the National Infrastructure Commission for Wales, we're piloting a new model of governance that, very literally, gives Nature a voice. While the current Public Appointments process doesn't permit a formal role for a Nature Guardian, we've created an informal arrangement that allows an advisor to act in that capacity. It's a practical workaround that puts ecological insight at the heart of our decisions, and a first step towards reimagining Nature not as a stakeholder to be consulted, but as a presence to be represented.

The sentiment here is common to all those who've adopted the move. While we recognise the limits of our own influence, and we might not be able to affect change at the highest level (yet!), we can kick-start that change within our own organisations – no matter how small, and with however many workarounds are necessary to make it possible.

When we first launched NOTB, something about it felt quite subversive. We were able to usher in the Rights of Nature despite governments not doing so themselves. If, in the space of only a few years, we have already come this far, then we have moved past subversion. We might think we are hidden inside a giant wooden Trojan horse but, in reality, the doors are wide open.

5

Heather: A Cultural Shift

We learn from the histories of the vegetable kingdom that Calluna vulgaris – the generally accepted botanical term for Heather – has a wide distribution throughout European countries, and in other parts of the world. But so closely has the word Heather become associated with Scotland, that whenever we hear it spoken, or see it written, the fancy instinctively roams to the 'land of brown heath and shaggy wood,' the beauty of whose stern mountains, softened with their autumnal vesture of purple and brown blending in every-varying and never exhausted tints, has baffled the painter's genius, enchanted the poet's vision, and inspired monarch and peasant alike to sing its praises. (*The Heather in Lore, Lyric and Lay*, Wallace, 1903)

From cathedrals to can-openers

If Nature on the Board (NOTB) and other ideas like it are to succeed, then it will be because they're not just commentaries on culture, or reactions to it, but plot drivers within it. They are narratives in action – both part of the change, but also catalysts for further change. They tell the story by *being* the story – prompting a cultural shift that is necessary for longer-term thinking.

The term 'cathedral thinking' dates back to times when architects were asked to design cathedrals that wouldn't be complete within their own lifetimes. Como Cathedral took over 400 years to complete and Barcelona's Sagrada Familia is still a work in progress, a century after Gaudi's death.

I've heard NOTB described as a 'cathedral idea' for precisely this reason: that its impacts will likely only be felt after our time. Less kindly, I've also heard it described as 'an exercise in futility'. Perhaps all cathedral thinking seems futile in the short term. There are stories of cathedrals in the UK where those who built them planted oak trees nearby so that by the time the structure needed repair, there would be suitable material to hand. To some of the people building the cathedral, planting those oaks may have seemed futile. Even after a hundred years, had the cathedral needed repair before the oaks were mature, their planting would still have seemed futile. But if you see the planting of oak trees for what it is – just the planting of oak trees, regardless of whether or not they ever repair a cathedral – then their planting is not futile. And neither is the *story* of their planting. The story of their planting reframes the timescales that it's possible to think within. It also builds a bridge between people who are centuries apart. It helps us think bigger, and more broadly, and more beautifully.

I've also heard NOTB described as a can-opener of an idea. A can-opener doesn't need to look far into the future, it needs only crack open a can – and with the lid off, any number of emergent ideas can pour out.

But the *much bigger* cathedral idea, the *much bigger* can-opener idea, is the persistent idea kept alive across millennia – often by indigenous people – that Nature has inalienable rights. It is this idea that is inspiring modern story-tellers to recreate their realities and provide us all with new lenses with which to relate to the world around us.

In all likelihood, the biggest impacts of NOTB won't be felt within any one business or organisation – but throughout culture as newer stories start to emerge, norms shift and language changes to accommodate a much bigger, much broader, more beautiful narrative.

Credit where it's due

If we are to change the story, we need not only to introduce new language and new ideas, but also to replace other, more unhelpful, terms. I find the term 'natural resources' particularly unhelpful given its implication that whatever Nature creates is simply a resource for human activity. The truth is that Nature plays its part in literally everything we do, everything we create, everything we pass off as our own.

Consider this book …

First, its physical aspects: If you are reading a printed copy of it, Nature provided the material for the paper. Nature provided the source material for the ink (even if it is printed with 'synthetic' inks, not 'natural' inks). Nature provided the material for the binding (whether it is glued or stitched). And even if you're reading a digital format of this book, there is not a piece of the device upon which you're reading it that didn't first originate in Nature (even if it has since been passed through multiple 'man-made' processes).

Now, its more abstract aspects: In David Abrams' *Spell of the Sensuous*, he argues that language itself emerged from Nature – its sounds, its structure, its symbolic meaning, and later the marks that became our written alphabets, enabling us to capture all of that in such a way that we can speak across space and time with people we may never meet. Through its beauty outside of us, Nature also creates awe and wonder within us. And Nature also provided the tools – *our beings* – to somehow knit all of this together into an idea that Anne managed to articulate as 'What if Nature *really* was the boss?' What was outside influenced what was inside, caused an utterance of sounds that echoed around the inside of our heads – bone-chambers formed from the very same stuff that inspired those sounds in the first place – and were instantly translated into something meaningful and new.

Nature has its fingerprints all over this book – and yet when I asked the publishers whether Nature could be named as its author, I was told this wasn't possible. We have created systems where, despite Nature's involvement in every aspect of our lives, we cannot credit the natural world even if we want to – much less pay it for what it provides. But even this is changing.

Earth Percent is an organisation co-founded by Brian Eno to address exactly this issue within the music industry. If the argument that Nature ought to be credited as an author of books remains a little clumsy, it's much less awkward to point to how Nature is directly involved with music production.

Nature provides so many of the materials still used to create instruments: wood, skin, hair and even our own larynxes. So many artists turn to Nature for inspiration – either 'just' as a space within which to create or as subject matter for their songs and lyrics. Nature also creates its own music, from the rhythms of rain and the hushing of the ocean to a bird's song – and so entrenched is this idea of Nature as musician that ancient Greeks proposed that the entire movement of the spheres was some grand symphony playing out all around us. Sometimes those sounds are either recreated – as in Benjamin Britten's 'Cuckoo' – or directly lifted and sampled, as has happened with the Common Loon's call in tracks by Sueno Latino, 808 State, Calvin Harris, Lady Gaga, Lana Del Rey, Nicki Minaj, Doja Cat and Michael Jackson. And then, of course, there is also the part that Nature – or *place* – plays in performances. Whichever way we look at it, Nature is at the heart of the music industry, but has never been paid.

Via the 'Sounds Right' initiative, 50 per cent of recording royalties from tracks that state 'Feat. Nature' will be donated to biodiversity conservation, as well as 63 per cent of royalties from ambient nature tracks. These royalties are then collected by Earth Percent and distributed to Nature conservation and restoration projects. The pilot of this project has so far contributed US$225,000 to conservation projects in Colombia – which though still a drop in the ocean, shows quite how much money could be flowing back towards Nature's recovery and restoration if we had better systems in place to recognise Nature's role in so much of what we take for granted.

Similarly, the United Nations-backed 'Lion's Share' initiative allows brands to contribute 0.5 per cent of their media spend towards wildlife conservation for every ad featuring an animal. Created with Mars (makers of Lion bars), it too highlights how much we have come to rely on powerful symbols from the natural world to turn a profit, but haven't (until now) thought to pay royalties to the rightful owners of those symbols: the animals themselves.

Just thinking about big cats alone, how much of these brand's successes are built on the 'borrowed' imagery of their feline brand icons? Lion (Mars and Peugeot), Jaguar, Puma, Cheetah (Cheetos), Tiger (Frosties and Kenzo), Cougar (Kuga/Ford), Leopard (Dolce & Gabbana), Lynx (Axe) …

It's likely you can draw up a similar list for all animals in the animal kingdom – and I wonder too how the growth of these brands might map against the decline of the animals themselves. Unless systems change, we are in danger of replacing all beings with abstract symbols of themselves, attached instead to products that played a part in their extinction.

Thankfully, creativity and reimagining is at the heart of a new story – one that Nature is also co-authoring – and it is against this backdrop that NOTB is not only spreading through the business world, but through culture too. Its seeds catch the wind – as heather's seeds do in the intermediate phase of ecological succession – and I've been as surprised as anyone to see where this idea has taken root.

Transforming capitalism

In May 2022, as we were entering the final months of figuring out how to make NOTB a reality, a timely and prescient exhibition opened in London's Barbican: Our Time on Earth.

When Anne and I visited, we felt, again, that great sense of inevitability. It did exactly as we'd done. It asked a lot of questions. Questions such as: 'Is it right to put a price on the free services that plants, animals and ecosystems offer humanity?', 'Should a river bring a legal action for compensation against the factory that pollutes it?' and 'How do we share wealth with non-human others?'. Through art, design and storytelling, the exhibition made accessible a conversation that can sometimes remain either esoteric or academic. It was yet another example of so many different people driving at the much bigger idea of *how* we integrate the Rights of Nature into our everyday lives, in so many different – but often overlapping – ways.

One of the exhibition's ideas seems to underpin so many others, and is one that it is impossible not to eventually arrive at: 'Why we need interspecies money' by Jonathan Ledgard. In the exhibition's notes he writes:

> It makes no sense that the market economy puts money into ores, promissory notes and blocks of computer code, but not into the continuance of rare, complex and ancient biological life (regardless of how difficult this is). There is an urgent need for a novel central bank to be mandated to issue a central bank digital currency that can be held by non-human life forms: in other words, an interspecies money.

He explains how 'The Bank for Other Species' will mint a 'Life Mark' and predicts that by 2030, many billions of dollars will be held in Life Marks – which other species will be able to spend in ways that best increase their own chances of survival. He goes on to say:

> We are at a tipping point in our evolutionary history. Other species occupy a peripheral place in our consciousness. We seldom think about their needs, or how they move through the world. This will change. Over the next decade, we will begin to develop a new ethics and economics that take better account of non-humans. They will not be persons to us, but neither will they any longer be things.

A year or so later, Kate Raworth – author of *Doughnut Economics* – took part in an episode of Radio 4's 'Start the Week' titled 'Democratic capitalism – marriage on the rocks'. In it, she defines capitalism as 'an economic system that prioritises, above all, delivering profit for the owners of wealth' and later references Faith In Nature appointing Nature to its board as 'one of the ways businesses with a purpose are transforming capitalism'.

If this is true, it's because I actually believe we *are* thinking more and more of other species' needs. We *are* recognising them as persons. And one of those needs is abundantly clear: to recompense Nature for its losses. The price that all Nature – including us – has paid for capitalism (as we've known it until now) is staggering. But if Nature *had* been paid for what it provides, then it too would be an 'owner of wealth'. If we take Nature as a whole, then it would undoubtedly be the *largest* 'owner of wealth'. And, whereas human shareholders continually need to reinvest in order to grow their share of wealth – always having to balance the books of incomings against outgoings – Nature simply produces its own investments. Nature is its own source of wealth. Money *does* grow on trees. It runs in rivers and through the veins of all beings. It lurks in ancient, fossilised remains and in the depths of the planet. So if we can somehow crack the code of how to remunerate Nature for what it produces, Nature's potential earnings are limitless. It is an infinite source of wealth that can continually be invested back into itself for its own survival ...

At no point throughout the creation of NOTB did we actually discuss capitalism, let alone transforming it. But it seems that many people are coming to the same conclusions: that when we realign around true purpose, the most powerful tools available to protect Nature are those same tools that have, in the past, been used against Nature. Creativity sometimes dances around the edges of more 'serious' subjects such as the law, banking and business governance – but it is within all of these that we can tackle not just the symptoms, but the cause. We can turn harmful ideas of 'ownership' on their heads – whether through hacking the intellectual property systems that credit the artist sampling the Common Loon but not the Common Loon itself, or the financial institutions that have made humans the only 'owners of wealth' and therefore the sole beneficiaries of capitalism. And we can each do our small part without having to rethink an entire system, because so many ideas are converging around a new (/old!) Nature-centric way of being. Together they form a clear and coherent worldview, and one that is far more fun to imagine, because it is based on health, wealth (for all) and, as Kate Raworth puts it, 'thriving'.

That Apple ad

One of the challenges of NOTB is showing what it really looks like. In reality, it *looks* much the same as any other board meeting. The difference is really in how it *feels*. Still, sharing the story of something that happens behind closed doors is, obviously, difficult.

But in September 2023, Apple made it a little easier when they put out an ad in which Mother Nature joined the tech giant's board for a '2030 Status' meeting. If you've not seen it, it goes a bit like this:

> Tim Cook and the Apple board shuffle about nervously as they wait for Mother Nature to join them. There is a lot of muttering about the 'weather'. Somebody hides a sad looking plant. Then, amidst a flurry of birds taking flight, Mother Nature (played by Octavia Spencer) appears. She seems generally sceptical, proclaiming this is the third corporate social responsibility meeting she's attended that day and asks 'So who wants to disappoint me first?' The board make their case for all the good things they're doing: eliminating all plastics from their packaging by the end of 2025, using 100 per cent recycled aluminium in all the enclosures of their Macbooks, Apple TVs and Apple Watches and phasing out leather in their iPhone cases. They're also planting forests, trying to save the Tropical Savanna, shifting to 100 per cent renewable energy, reducing their water usage, etc, etc, etc. ... Then Tim Cook presents Mother Nature with their latest Apple Watch, which is 100 per cent carbon balanced. Mother Nature looks a little less sceptical than before, but insists she 'wants to see more of this'. 'We will', says Tim Cook. There is a face-off between the two. Mother Nature's eyes say 'I've heard it all before'. Tim Cook's eyes say 'But we mean it'. And then Mother Nature leaves and says she'll see them all again next year.

To some involved with NOTB, that ad was a slap in the face. Having worked so hard to (1) go beyond what could be perceived as marketing to implement real legal change and (2) so often make this case to anyone who claimed this was 'yet another piece of marketing', it felt like a death-knell for the still fledgling idea. Apple had implied that they had invited Mother Nature to their board without making any of the legal changes underpinning the idea. 'Share of voice = share of market' is a media catch-cry that means whoever spends the most, gains the most. The fear was that Apple would do the same with NOTB – that by spending millions, NOTB would come to be recognised as what Apple had made it – a piece of marketing. (And, by contrast, any attempts to make this a real, meaningful move would soon fizzle out …)

But, personally, I felt differently. To me, they'd done something we could never have done: they'd mainstreamed an idea at a Hollywood scale. They'd also given us something to point at, to explain what we'd done. Thanks to 'that Apple ad' we had a tool to explain what NOTB *is* and, in many more ways, what NOTB *is not*. So let's do just that. What's similar? (Spoiler: not much.) And what's different? (Spoiler: quite a lot.)

First, the similarities:

1. The funniest, truest, similarity is that this first meeting with Mother Nature does actually remind me of Faith In Nature's first ever meeting with Nature. It was, by far, the worst board meeting I'd ever witnessed. That sense of being judged is real. You *do* feel exposed and you *do* feel vulnerable. So, to over-correct, there is a desperate clamouring to present the best versions of yourself (and to feel embarrassed at how thirsty the office plants look, as if they must represent much greater misdeeds elsewhere in the business). At the back of my mind was a voice asking 'What have we done?!' The result, obviously, is a quite chaotic first encounter.
2. The other obvious similarity is the embodiment of Nature as a human. That's actually quite helpful because it helps explain the guardian function detailed earlier in this book. Theoretically, it is possible that Nature's guardians could be more-than-human, but right now, that seems a long way off.
3. Perhaps the biggest similarity, albeit alluded to only in a slightly comic way, is that Nature really is a stakeholder. This ad does acknowledge that there is a greater presence 'in the room' as we go about our business. There is something else far more precious than profits to be considered.
4. But apart from that, the only other similarities are the obvious board meeting tropes: a table in an office, around which sit a (presumably) privileged set of people making decisions that impact the wider world far away from their safe, clean and

sterile boardroom – a place designed to make it easy to pretend this isn't the case.

Now, the differences:

1. To be completely clear, the biggest and most important difference in all of this is that this is just an ad. It is the dramatisation of an idea that has genuinely been implemented elsewhere but without any of the legal, corporate or structural changes necessary to make it anything more than this. It is a piece of theatre that nods towards the Rights of Nature without actually doing what the movement needs, which is to recognise those rights with genuine legal change. To say you work for Mother Nature without actually making any legal changes to make that true is … *not true*.

2. Although the ad does remind me of the chaos of the first ever meeting with Nature present, by the time the second meeting came around, those feelings had dissipated, exactly as we knew they would. The reality is that we'd been working on NOTB for almost 18 months before that meeting, so were confident in the move. All the nerves and feelings of vulnerability were really just monkey-mind nonsense and chatter. The beauty of NOTB is that Nature doesn't just leave after the first meeting. Nature stays. Nature listens. Nature shares. Nature's guardians work to understand our challenges as we work to understand how we might be impacting the natural world. This is not a one night stand, or an annual fling, but the entering into of a deep and meaningful relationship.

3. While a desire to please is normal, it's also fundamentally flawed. It is flawed because to seek approval assumes an element of judgement. The truth is NOTB is not about judging or being judged, but of opening up a dialogue and starting a new way of interrelating. Nature – or its guardians – are free to judge us, but to what end? NOTB is a tool for making better informed decisions that take the natural world into account. There is already an acknowledgement within that we are, obviously, not perfect. None of us is. So it's about working together to be better going forward. Nature does not sit on our board as some authoritarian green police force. Nature sits on our board as a guide, as an ally

and as a legally recognised stakeholder. The 'So who wants to disappoint me first?' line is anathema to the entire idea.

4. Apple's ad also muddies the water between having Nature on the board and having a Sustainability Director. While Octavia Spencer is referred to as 'Mother Nature', if you re-cut the ad and referred to her instead as 'Octavia, Sustainability Director', nothing else would change. Talk of carbon emissions, materials, water usage, and so on is already within the scope of a sustainability director – and Faith In Nature already has one of those in addition to Nature as a director. Of course, Nature too has an interest in carbon footprints and targets and all the stuff sustainability people speak of. But the bigger point is that Nature is there to input on all decisions and aspects of the business, bringing an ecocentric lens to the otherwise anthropocentric business world. Nature, in our case, speaks of so much more. Nature speaks of imagination, of a rights discourse, of systems change, of ways of seeing and being that are not only measured, but felt.

5. And while Mother Nature's embodiment as a human is similar to ours, it is also very different. We are not saying our Nature guardians *are* Nature (although they are, of course, part of Nature). We're saying they're guardians of Nature, working in Nature's best interests. In that sense, the people we appoint must bring some great expertise and insight into the natural world that is otherwise not present in the boardroom. By contrast, what we see with Apple's embodiment of Mother Nature is really just a creative treatment. Octavia Spencer has been cast, presumably, because she's a wonderful actor and because she's famous. And obviously, this makes complete sense given the context – because this is a slick piece of theatre.

6. There is also the difference in language. I have already mentioned why we choose to say 'Nature', not 'Mother Nature'. Largely, it's cultural. It's also to ground the idea in the everyday – so that there is one less barrier to overcome.

7. And then, there is the really, really big difference that this depiction of NOTB is trying to flog another Apple product. And that's fine – that's what ads are for. But NOTB itself is not trying to sell anything. It's trying to fix a business culture of riding roughshod over the interests of the natural world.

And, yes, it is in the interests of the move for the companies that adopt it to be commercially successful – but if they are, it will be because they're great companies, selling great products or services, in an ethical way that customers recognise as being critical to the future health of the planet.

An environmental lawyer close to NOTB described the ad as 'the worst thing that could have happened to the movement'. I understand their disappointment and frustration – but the ad guy in me still disagrees.

Perhaps it's because I did not devote my career to justice, or to meaningful change – to whatever extent that came, that came later. I still really, really love ads. I love the craft, the creativity, the production and the performance of good ads. I also love the curiosity of people in ad-land. I love that they take inspiration from anywhere and everywhere. They surface what is interesting, culturally 'sticky' or beautiful. And yes, they then twist those things into ways of selling stuff. But, well, that's the industry.

I prefer to take this in the spirit it's possibly (perhaps even unconsciously) intended. This ad does what so many other ads before it have done. It 'borrows' an idea. Often, advertising's references are film treatments, directors' styles, art movements, songs, dance routines or sub-culture movements. But sometimes they're philosophies, big ideas or just small, tender observations of everyday life. In this instance – on whatever level – their reference is NOTB. It's proof that the conversation has reached Tim Cook and Octavia Spencer and the millions of people who have since seen the ad.

My only real complaint with the whole thing is that despite Mother Nature saying she'll see them all again 'next year', she hasn't yet returned. Apple haven't (yet) appointed Nature to their board – nor is there any real suggestion that they ever will – but they have amplified the whole movement in a way very few other companies ever could.

Reaching across audiences

Of all the places I hadn't anticipated finding NOTB – and certainly not the *first* place to feature it as a storyline – it was in the long-running BBC radio soap, *The Archers* (which, for the uninitiated, revolves around the small fictional community of 'Ambridge' in rural England and has been running since 1951). My perception of *The Archers* was that nothing very much ever happens in their bucolic corner of radio-land – and yet, in the episode in question, Justin Elliott returns from a sustainability conference and proclaims that he's discovered a new idea in which Nature is made a director. Given Stella Pryor's interest in improving soil health, he proposes she act as Nature's guardian on the board of 'Borchester Land', a company recently bought by his private equity company, 'Damara Capital'. (How wrong I was about nothing much happening in Ambridge!)

I'm glad that Justin found his sustainability conference so useful. Personally, I find many of them quite frustrating. In creative conferences, you can't present to a room full of people unless you've got actual, tangible creative output to share. But in many sustainability conferences, it seems acceptable to speak for an hour without ever getting to an idea – let alone something the audience can take away and get on and *do*.

By contrast, if there's one group of people who embody this no-nonsense approach to doing and not just talking, it's Karla, CC, Hiva, Aurvi, Joaquin, Skye, Ruby and Joseph – the stars of the Damon Gameau film, *Future Council*. In it, these eight brilliant kids go on a road-trip of big businesses, meeting the CEOs of major multinationals and challenging them on their lack of action.

As part of the film, they also meet Brontie and me in a glass box in the forest where we explain what NOTB is, how it works and why it matters – but, in truth, they were already way ahead of us. We didn't need to tell these kids *why* this matters. What they want to know is why more adults in the business world can't already see this. Why they pretend as if it doesn't matter. Why it must be them who inherit this mess, by which time it might be too late. They are sharp-minded, kind-hearted and a stark contrast to so many of the professional talkers who owe them so much more. And yet, despite everything they foresee coming down the road, they remain bright and light and they filled my heart with hope.

Even before its global release, the film has already featured at New York Climate Week and screened at the United Nations General Assembly – and, thanks to those children and that film,

NOTB will reach the eyes and ears of exactly the people who really can give Nature a voice at the highest level.

Mother Nature in the Boardroom is another short film by Sea Change Project, narrated by Craig Foster of *My Octopus Teacher*. It too screened at Climate Week as well as at OCEANS20, the first engagement group focused on the ocean in the G20. In it, Dr Jane Goodall gives voice to Mother Nature, asking: 'Do I have a seat at the table? I am, after all, the biggest shareholder ...'

That message is fast landing with all those who need to hear it. The question remains, what will they do with it? Those who hear of it might still not see the immediate need for it. Nor might they see its immediate benefits even if they do implement it. But if NOTB was partly created to ensure directors can't be wilfully blind to the impact of their decisions, then the same is true for everyone who has now encountered the idea. If they continue *not* to give Nature a seat at the table, then they do so knowing that it *is* possible.

They say that the best time to plant a tree was 20 years ago, but the second best time to plant a tree is now. If Karla, CC, Hiva, Aurvi, Joaquin, Skye, Ruby and Joseph planted trees today, a young forest could still grow within their lifetimes. The same applies for NOTB and all other Nature-centric ideas. The best time to have implemented them was decades ago. But the second best time is now.

Those who do might never see their benefits, but there is a chance that Karla, CC, Hiva, Aurvi, Joaquin, Skye, Ruby and Joseph might. So too might the billions of other invisible stakeholders – all of whom we collectively refer to as 'Nature' – who currently have no say in the decisions that impact all life on Earth.

A message from Skye Neville

Skye Neville is one of the eight brilliant stars of *Future Council* – those eight brilliant kids, cast from thousands of equally brilliant kids – for whom this shift is not a fantasy but a necessity.

When I mentioned the National Infrastructure Commission for Wales' report on mitigating flood risks, I also mentioned Fairbourne – one of the first villages in the UK that will be underwater when sea levels rise. Decisions have already been made not to intervene in Fairbourne's future, effectively writing it off as a lost cause and the media describing its inhabitants as 'the UK's first climate refugees'. As a resident of Fairbourne, Skye is one of those future climate refugees.

She is also the inspirational founder of 'Kids Against Plastic Tat' (KAPtat). It is people like Skye for whom this is most real – so I described to her the type of person who might be reading this book, and asked what she might like to say to that person. These are her brilliant, unedited words, to you …

Hi, my name is Skye Neville, 14-year-old climate activist and founder of KAPtat – the campaign to get rid of cheap plastic tat from kids comics and magazines. I first met Simeon during the filming of *Future Council* and was blown away by the idea of having Nature as a board member, a simple solution which could have a huge positive impact on the Nature Crisis.

All around us Nature is calling out in distress, but many people and businesses, cannot or will not choose to listen. 'I'm suffering' she cries as we continue to destroy habitats and ecosystems at an alarming rate. 'I'm hurting' says Nature as we continue to burn fossil fuels to power our never ending appetites for consumption. 'I'm ANGRY' she shouts as violent storms, floods and weather events increase in frequency and intensity. The warning calls are there but business finds it hard to listen, the never ending drive for growth and money shouts louder, selfishness and greed block out Nature's voice.

Nature has been removed from the cities, removed from the places where decisions are made and removed from businesses. Decisions to clear forests and jungles, to mine sea beds and drill on pristine arctic tundras are taken in board rooms, in big cities, in different countries. The decision makers will have never even seen the areas whose destruction they sign off in the name of profit and shareholder value. Advertisers and marketing businesses feed the monster that is consumption, further drowning out Nature's cries, masking her voice and confusing her message with Greenwashing.

When Nature shouts, the huge destructive power is heard and felt but not in the boardrooms where the decisions were made. The resulting catastrophes are always somewhere else, affecting other people, in other parts of the world. Often the poorest communities with the smallest voices are hit hardest, but business chooses not to see, or hear, or care. And even if the business does hear, for many change is too challenging, it's far easier just to carry on as normal, feeding the monster that is greed, money and consumption.

Reconnect with Nature and you can begin to respect and restore. Reconnect and work with Nature rather than against and opportunities and solutions will become more obvious. Place Nature on the board and decisions seem simple. Why does any magazine need a plastic wrapper? Why does a bunch of bananas need a plastic bag? Cucumbers, carrots, apples all wrapped in plastic. Why do we use so much energy to build rigs, to drill, to extract, to transport and refine oil, to then produce single use plastics? Excess packaging, cheap plastic tat, novelty 'gifts', sparkly, shiny glittery things that nobody needs or even wants, are all produced from the oil industry. Essentially they are producing a constant stream of literal rubbish with no interest in what happens after that one, single use.

If you haven't watched *The Lorax* then I suggest you do, it beautifully reflects the world's situation as we destroy vast areas of Nature, exploiting it until there is nothing left, before abandoning it and moving on to repeat the process somewhere else. All to produce products that nobody wants and nobody needs … unless the advertising monster tells you otherwise!

Future businesses simply need to care about Nature and Sustainability. Not the corporate greenwashing type of pretend care, proudly showcasing and supporting an environmental project whilst quietly continuing to wreck the planet. We need real care. Care for true sustainability – meeting the needs of the present without compromising the ability of future generations to meet their own needs.

Care and responsibility for the entire life of a product, from its design and production all the way through to repair and ultimately recycle. If a product cannot be fully recycled it should never be made. Polluters, in all their forms, should be forced to clean up their mess. Blaming the consumers and attempting to recycle are not the solutions, we have to turn off the tap of production and make the polluter pay.

Nature needs to have a voice at the table where the decisions are made, and every decision needs to consider the impacts. A sustainable future needs business and society to be more responsible, more ethical, fairer and kinder.

I don't know much about running a business, but I know that if we want to protect Nature we need to make positive changes. These changes can be simple, use a refillable bottle, recycle, eat less meat, buy less stuff.

Reconnect with Nature and listen to her voice when you make choices – seriously no magazine needs a single use plastic wrapper!!!!

6

Bluebell: A Future with Nature at the Table

I do not think I have ever seen anything more beautiful than the bluebell ... I know the beauty of our Lord by it. Its inscape is strength and grace ... William Turner in *The Names of Herbes* of 1548 was the first to record the bluebell as we know it, and half a century later the herbalist John Gerard named it Hyacinthus anglicus, 'for that it is thought to grow more plentifully in England than elsewhere'. Which it does, all over Britain during April and May in deciduous woodland. The bluebell, beauty of the springtime woods with its elongated bell flowers on a drooping leafless stem, can vary in colour from azure to lilac, even to a pure white form that flourishes in my cottage garden among the springtime bulbs. (*Britain's Wild Flowers*, Richardson, 2017)

Clara Abbott and Lettie Pate Whitehead

Clara Abbott was the first woman appointed to the board of any major company. She served two terms as a director of Abbott Laboratories from 1900 to 1908 and later from 1911 to 1924. There was then a ten-year wait before Lettie Pate Whitehead became the second woman appointed to the board of a major corporation. She became a director of Coca-Cola in 1934.

Until their appointments, women too were major stakeholders of companies' decision-making and yet also denied a voice and a vote on those decisions that impacted them. When Clara Abbott and Lettie Pate Whitehead were finally appointed to their positions, we have no way of knowing exactly how they governed. There are no public minutes detailing every decision they made or records of how they voted, but it is surely the fact they were able to break through at all – in an entirely male corporate world – that must remain their greatest achievement.

In all likelihood, other men on other boards will have asked why Abbott Laboratories and Coca-Cola needed a woman on their boards. What, they might have asked, could Clara Abbott and Lettie Pate Whitehead offer that they couldn't? What decisions would they make that men couldn't have made without them? I can imagine the grumblings through the corporate corridors of the time: 'An exercise in futility ...'

That it is difficult to pinpoint their specific noteworthy actions misses the much, *much* bigger point that there have since been millions of micro-decisions made by women in the boardroom that have inevitably led to better lives for women *and* men. And their being in the boardroom has also, inevitably, led to men making more informed decisions that better take into account the needs and wants of women. The balance of men and women working *together* will have benefited everyone.

Of course, all of this is blindingly obvious. Likewise, so are the parallels. Surely it must hold for all stakeholders that to be given a seat at the table significantly boosts the chances of them improving their own wellbeing? And surely those stakeholders themselves are best placed to speak in their own best interests?

To suggest otherwise strikes me as either extraordinarily arrogant, ignorant or, perhaps, even malicious. If we can clearly see that there is a stakeholder affected by our decisions but we refuse to give them equal stakeholder rights, then what is that if not an act of oppression?

To invite Nature into the conversation is to recognise Nature's right to input. It is to recognise that Nature *already* inputs. If through inviting Nature into the conversations and really, actually listening, we arrive at the same decisions regardless, then that can only be a *good* thing. It means that other directors are already thinking in Nature-positive ways and that, now, they can have those decisions validated and endorsed by experts who have devoted their lives to the natural world.

Not everything needs to take a radically different path because we invite another stakeholder into the conversation. Perhaps the most important part of that conversation is just asking permission, consent or advice. Perhaps that *is* the radical change.

But, really, what are the chances that through engaging with another stakeholder, nothing changes at all? What are the chances that nothing improves? Had Clara Abbott and Lettie Pate Whitehead not been given a seat at the table, and had they not paved the way for all the women who have since also served on boards, what are the chances that all male boards would have made the same decisions as have been reached by boards where men and women work together? That the world today would be exactly as it is? That women would remain shut out of decision-making but, through some extraordinary coincidence, men had proven themselves capable of understanding women just as well as women understand themselves? That without women in the boardroom, all boards everywhere would take women's best interests into account regardless?

(Even *with* women in the boardroom this isn't the case. Take the gender pay gap, for example. It's around 7 per cent in the UK, while approximately 40 per cent of board positions are held by women. Imagine how much worse the pay gap would likely be if there were even fewer women on boards. Likewise, imagine how much better – or perhaps non-existent – the pay gap would be if there were *more* women on boards.)

Hopefully we don't need to imagine a parallel scenario in which Nature continues to be denied its stakeholder rights. There was a ten-year gap between the appointment of the first woman on the board of a company and the second. There was only a year between Nature being named director of one company and then another. Hopefully, in the fullness of time, it won't be the decisions made by either of these directorships that really matters but, rather, the conditions created for a more Nature-centric society through the millions of micro-decisions made by Nature (as director) in all of the boardrooms across the lands ...

Perhaps, one day, all directors will be better placed to act in the best interests of the natural world. Perhaps we will have developed governance structures, protocols and systems that mean we can all make legitimate claims to being 'Nature-positive' or 'Nature guardians'. That is as it *should* be. For now, Nature on the Board (NOTB) is an intervention – designed to help get us to that point. My hope is that, one day, everything in this book should seem so obvious it need barely be said.

And yet, we have already been saying this since time immemorial. Nearly 200 years ago, Victor Hugo said: 'How sad to think that Nature speaks and mankind doesn't listen.' *The Animals' Lawsuit Against Humanity* is a recent English translation of a tale penned in Hebrew in the 1400s that drives towards this same idea. It is based on an even older text – *The Case of the Animals Versus Man* – written in Iraq in 960. Doubtless, there are fables and folklore much, much older that make this exact same point, over, and over, and over ...

We can't take anything for granted.

Bluebells (on the moor)

In imagining a future in which the boardroom is (re)wilded – its transformation complete – it is tempting to reach for an oak tree as a symbol of late stage succession; some mighty giant that has stood strong and tall over centuries, bearing witness to the world that has changed around it.

But there are other, more delicate, climax species. A bluebell won't stand a thousand years, but a splash of bluebells will return each year, continuing to flourish and spread wherever conditions allow – mostly in ancient woodland and other special, rare habitats.

Famously, they carpet forest floors and each one is delicate and beautiful in its own right – but we can afford to lose a few when there are thousands of others to replace them.

We need to approach Nature-positive ideas in the same way. We should embrace a spirit of experimentation, of freedom and play. This, to me, is the opportunity that a more Nature-centric culture presents. The sustainability conversation has become so heavy that, by contrast, a conversation about (and with!) Nature is so much lighter. It is rich with opportunity.

Most days, Anne and I walk out of our back gate onto miles of moorland. Bluebells don't grow on the moor, but ideas blossom as we wander. The moor – overgrazed and devoid of wildlife – is the boardroom all over again. The closer we get to it, the more something seems amiss. It's common-land, though technically still private land, owned by a barony for the past 900 years. Half of all land in England is owned by less than 1 per cent of the population. All land in the UK is owned either by humans and/or corporate bodies or trusts (run by humans). Even if some of that land is given to conservation, no other species has any legal say in how it is managed.

As I approach writing the end of this book, I asked Anne to walk with me again. Clara Abbott and Lettie Pate Whitehead had paved the way for Anne's position on a board. She had paved the way for Nature's. How, I asked, can more people cause radical change? With the same clarity that led her to ask 'What if Nature really was the boss?', she laid out her thinking in three steps:

1. Do whatever necessary to cause the 'mind-flip'. Create a new lens for seeing the world.
2. Dare to ask: Why are we doing it this way? And why are we *still* doing it this way?
3. Realise we have the freedom to change it. So much is just make-believe.

Then, she paused, and with the directness of somebody raised in the Australian bush, added a fourth:

4. Stop talking. Get on and do it.

Kill your darlings

Part of every creative process is knowing when to 'kill your darlings'. It's the time when we realise that what seemed to work before no longer works. We reach that point when – no matter how we try to refine it, reshape it or repackage it – the idea simply no longer fits.

Systems design is no different. Systems designed to work exclusively for one species – making us the only 'owners of wealth' – have already failed. They've never worked for the wider natural world, and now they're proving not to work for us either.

And so we are left with little choice. 'Killing your darlings' is painful. It takes tremendous effort to give up. And it takes resilience, flexibility and drive to try something else. But it is also incredibly cathartic.

It's also a time to question what our efforts are really for. If we are to reorganise around Nature-positive systems, then underlying every Nature-positive initiative ought to be the intention to create a more equitable outcome for all beings. If we can gather around that purpose with integrity, but without the need to save face, then we can free ourselves from ideas that have come to shape us (even though we might think it is us who shape them). When we start to realise we are trapped by certain ideas, enslaved to making the unworkable work, it's liberating to start anew. And that's when we can start to have fun again.

Nature can even show us *how* to kill our darlings. Nature's own systems are far more efficient than any human-made system – and inbuilt within Nature's systems is a continuous renewal. It happens throughout the natural world, over and over again.

Nature doesn't do this to self-sabotage or because what worked yesterday wasn't right for yesterday. Nature does this to succeed. So that the ideas needed for tomorrow are ready for tomorrow. Likewise, so must we.

So why do we remain so rigid in our own systems? There are no laws of physics that dictate we must do things one way and not another. To ask *Why are we still doing it this way?* is not to deal with some immovable object – even if we must, at times, deal with immovable people. But why? Where's the resistance?

The answer to *Why are we still doing it this way?* will usually be either money, power or 'heritage'. In other words, 'because we've always done things this way'. But there are enough of us now who see those reasons are no longer enough. We see that what's at stake is so much greater, more precious and more valuable.

That's the role of 'lichen' – to change not the world itself, but the way we see the world. To kick-start the process of ecological succession so that we might, finally, arrive at *this* part. The part where there are enough of us who see the world in such a way that, together, we can create those new systems that Nature so desperately needs.

If Nature really was the boss ...

We might agree that, at a macro level, the idea that needs reworking is anthropocentrism. But how do we translate that into the everyday? Into the fabric of our daily lives? Simply, I think, by asking better questions – and trusting that somebody out there will be able to help us find better answers.

NOTB started by asking a simple question. *How might one business change if Nature had a voice and a vote?* That quickly grew into *How might business (as a whole) change if Nature had a voice and a vote?* Today, I'm starting to wonder *How might we (as a society) change if Nature had a voice and a vote?*

Of course, I don't know what I don't know. In other words, I cannot ask the right questions for areas I know nothing about. But perhaps you can. Or, perhaps with Nature's guardians alongside you, you might find opportunities for change where, perhaps, nobody has thought to look before.

Perhaps a good way to frame those questions is:

> If Nature really was the boss ... [insert the bit you are uniquely placed to ask here]

What follows are 60 'silly' questions I prepared earlier so that you might feel less 'silly' asking yours. They're just half-thoughts and questions that I deliberately gave myself no more than an hour to write. You might find them helpful. Or unhelpful. Idealistic, or naïve. Radical, or ridiculous. But hopefully they'll spark something. At the end of the list is space for 60 of your own. Give yourself no more than an hour. Ask from the heart, not from the head (there will be plenty of time for the head to get involved, figuring out the detail, later).

If Nature really was the boss ...

> ... *what would it say about land ownership?*
> ... *what legal structures could be created to protect land in perpetuity?*
> ... *would you give up one square metre of your garden to achieve its aims?*
> ... *how might it reform planning laws?*
> ... *what might it designate a National Park?*
> ... *how could it ensure housing for all (human and kin alike)?*
> ... *would 'regenerative covenants' be included in house sales?*
> ... *could a portion of land tax be paid for Nature regeneration?*
> ... *how might land taxes change?*
> ... *could Nature Repair Liability replace Chancel Repair Liability?*
> ... *shouldn't it sit in the House of Lords, as do 26 bishops?*
> ... *what new insurance products might it design?*
> ... *how might it change companies' bonus structures?*
> ... *how would it (re)design company structures?*
> ... *what would Nature-related key performance indicators look like?*
> ... *how would it (re)design work spaces?*
> ... *what would its people policy be?*
> ... *which new public holidays would it introduce?*
> ... *how would we celebrate those newly introduced public holidays?*
> ... *how would it (re)design hospitals?*
> ... *how would it (re)design the health service more broadly?*
> ... *what treatments might it prescribe?*
> ... *how would it define 'health'?*

… *how might national health include natural health?*
… *how would it (re)design care homes?*
… *what would a care home for Nature look like?*
… *could it introduce 'natural service' (rather than national service)?*
… *what might it ask of big pharma?*
… *what claims to proprietary property might it make?*
… *how might it ration its 'resources'?*
… *would it price its 'resources' and would Earth Overshoot Day affect its pricing?*
… *what might it define a healthy 'stock level' of its resources?*
… *how might accounting methods change?*
… *how might the school curriculum change?*
… *what changes to languages might we see?*
… *what stories might it commission?*
… *how might the media landscape change?*
… *what books might it publish?*
… *what achievements might it celebrate?*
… *who might it name Person of the Year?*
… *how might it make us all feel as though we belong?*
… *what would it say to the most sceptical?*
… *what could it do to be a better employer than any human before it?*
… *how might it encourage innovation?*
… *would it run its own grant programme?*
… *could it run its own lottery?*
… *where would it keep its money?*
… *who would control its bank account?*
… *would its bank account belong to one country, all countries or no country?*
… *how might those countries benefit economically?*
… *how would we pay into its bank account?*
… *where would it invest its funds?*
… *what would a good return on investment look like?*
… *would it establish its own funds?*
… *could we store our pensions in those funds?*

... would those funds pass to future generations (of all beings) if not spent within our lifetimes?
... what new industries might it create?
... who might it need to run them?
... what skills might those people need and where might they learn them?
... what skills could YOU teach them?

If Nature really was the boss ...

... _____

... _____

... _____

... _____

... _____

... _____

... _____

... _____

... _____

... _____

... _____

... _____

... _____

... _____

... _____

... _____

... _____

... _____

... _____

... _____

... _____

... _____

... _____

... _____

... _____

... _____

... _____

... _____

... _____

... _____

... _____

... _____

... _____

... _____

... _____

... _____

... _____

... _____

... _____

... _____

... _____

... _____

... _____

... _____

... _____

... _____

... _____

... _____

... _____

... _____

... _____

... _____

... _____

... _____

... _____

... _____

... _____

... _____

... _____

... _____

Perhaps you didn't quite get to 60, or perhaps you lost track of time and went way over. Maybe you'll want to do this again tomorrow. Or keep coming back to it. Maybe it's also helpful to reframe the question so that Nature isn't 'boss', but 'friend', 'equal' or, simply, 'a stakeholder'. Twist it until something in you unlocks or until you develop a relationship with it that feels more inspiring and truer to you.

Apply it to your area of specialism. Perhaps you're part of a team where you could run this exercise. That could be your company, a school, a university, a sports club, an association of which you're a member or wherever you volunteer your time. (Or perhaps you're Tim Cook, preparing for Mother Nature's return to the Apple boardroom. Perhaps you could all do this together?)

Does one question stand out? Does it lead to ten more? When you're ready, why not embrace the reimagining and pass this book on – filled with your questions – to somebody you think might have answers?

A voice and a vote

If 'working for the man' is what's gotten us into the mess we're in today, could a shift towards 'working for Nature' be what it takes to get us out?

To my mind, and to many people's minds, we must acknowledge Nature as the stakeholder that it so clearly is. When we do, we see that so many of our current systems are out of balance – just as is the natural world. And that while conservation efforts to restore biodiversity are heroic, we would restore balance to the natural world much quicker if we could restore balance to the systems within which we operate. If an organisation wants to signal its commitment towards recognising Nature as a stakeholder, then appointing Nature to its board is one of the simplest – but perhaps also most powerful – changes it can make.

Bringing Nature into your everyday life is proven to improve mental and physical wellbeing. I believe bringing Nature into your organisation can improve its wellbeing too. It can also be fun. And rewarding. And helpful. And wild. And creative. And equitable. And sensible. And practical. And pragmatic. And *successful*. Because it's in Nature's interest that this succeeds – for Nature as a whole, and the organisations that adopt it.

But none of this is about the idea itself, nor the mechanics of it, nor its underlying legal thinking or any of the fantastical ideas it leads to. If we get too caught up in all of that then we've lost sight of what this is truly about. This is about the wider natural world – the source not only of our wealth, but also of our joy, our healing, our *humanity*. But to feel all of that, we must also feel its pain right now. A pain so unbearable that the simple act of granting Nature a voice and a vote seems the very least we can do.

Index

A

Abbott, Clara 80, 81
Abrams, David, *Spell of the Sensuous* 63
advertising 3, 50, 68–72, 75–76
AI guardians 36–37
animal guardians 35–36
animal rights 9
*The Animals' Lawsuit Against
    Humanity* 80
Ansell, Brontie 11, 17, 19, 73
Apple's Mother Nature advert 68–72, 93
The Archers 73
Armitage, Simon 31
Arts and Humanities Research
    Council 56
arts organisations 55

B

Barrington Tops, New South
    Wales 4–5
Being There (Hal Ashby film) 7
Better Business Network 54–55
biodiversity funding 41–42
biodiversity loss 2, 41, 65, 75–77
bluebells 79, 82–83
boardroom environments 12–13
Bolivia 9
branding 5–8, 64–65
Brecon Beacons (Bannau
    Brycheiniog) 4, 57
business networks 54–55

C

Campylopus 15
Canada 22
The Case of the Animals Versus Man 82
cathedral thinking 62
charities 22, 53–54
Chiricahua Mountains, Arizona 47
civil assemblies 56

Clubb, David 59
Coelho, Paulo 46
Common Loon 64, 67
Commonwealth Climate and Law
    Initiative 31
Como Cathedral 62
Cook, Tim 68, 72, 93

D

Donaldson, Rene 47–49
Donaldson, Tony 47

E

Earth Day 2
Earth Law Center 10, 33
Earth Percent 64
Earth Species Project 36
ecological succession 13, 16, 33, 35
Ecuador 9, 30
Eno, Brian 64
environmental personhood 10, 11, 18

F

Fairbourne, mid Wales 59, 74–75
Faith In Nature
    brand identity 5–8
    making Nature a director *see* Nature
        on the Board (NOTB)
    choice of guardians 32–33, 35
    founding and ownership 2, 52
    products 2, 34, 39
    questioning approach 38–39
    supply chain 37–39
flood resilience 58–59
Foster, Craig 73
Friends of Cave Creek Canyon
    (FOCCC) 46, 47–50
Future Council (Damon Gameau
    film) 73–75

Future Everything arts organisation 55
Future Generations 51–52

G
Ganges river, India 33
gender pay gap 81
Global Alliance for the Rights
    of Nature 8
Goodall, Dr Jane 74
Gormley, Frieda 50–52
gorse 29
Gower Street charitable trust 53–54

H
heather 61
hills and mountains 4–5, 15, 47
Hopkins, Anne 2, 4, 4–5, 7–8, 11, 83
House of Hackney 50–52
Hugo, Victor 80

I
intellectual property systems 63–64, 67
interspecies money 65–66
Intradrive 52–53

J
Johnstone, Tom 58

K
Kids Against Plastic Tat
    (KAPtat) 75–77
Krznaric, Roman 54

L
land ownership 83
Lawyers for Nature 10–11, 20, 22, 25,
    33, 51
Ledgard, Jonathan 65–66
lichens 1, 13, 16
Lion's Share Fund 64
The Lorax (Chris Renaud film) 76
Lucocq, Helen 58

M
Marple, Sophie and Nick 53–54
Mars Inc 64–65
mind-flips 11, 83
mosses 15
Mother Nature in the Boardroom
    (Sea Change Project film) 74

Mount Melbourne, Antarctica 15
music industry, Nature's role in 64

N
National Infrastructure Commission
    for Wales 58–59
'natural resources', as term 63
Nature
    definitions and use of term 4, 26, 28
    human connection with 3, 5
    rights of 8–11
    threats to 2, 41, 65, 75–76
Nature on the Board (NOTB)
    development of idea 2, 7–11
    how it works
        overview 17–19
        decision-making 18–19, 27, 40
        guardianship model *see*
            Nature Guardians
        Nature as independent and
            external 18
        purpose clause 18, 21, 23–25
        transparency and accountability 19,
            27–28, 40–41
        underlying principle 12, 19–20
    legal framework 23–28
        overview 19–21
        composition of Board 26
        directors' meetings 26–27
        Non-Executive Director
            provisions 25–27
        objects clause 23–25
        'provide reasons' clause 27
        reporting obligations 28
    application and adaptation
        of concept
        general potential 22, 44, 46, 55
        arts organisations 55
        business networks 54–55
        charitable trusts 53–54
        civil assemblies 56
        flood resilience reports 58–59
        interior design companies 50–52
        manufacturing companies 52–53
        river catchment partnerships 57–58
        volunteer groups 47–50
        Apple advert compared 68–72
        as cathedral idea 62
        timing of adoption 53, 54
        potential in other jurisdictions 22
        potential in wider society 85–93
    Nature Guardians
        overview 29–31

advocacy differentiated 21
challenges of role 39, 40
choice of guardians 33–35
definition of term 26
diversity of perspectives 30–31
importance of role 41–42, 44
potential use of AI 36–37
procedural rights 26–27, 32, 39–40, 41
purpose of role 18, 29–30, 40, 42–43
as shared role 32–33
sustainability directors
    differentiated 71
tenure and removal 27, 32
time commitments 40
voices of other species 35–36
Neville, Skye 73, 74–77
New York Climate Week 73–74
New Zealand 22
non-governmental organisations 22

O
OCEANS20 74
Our Time on Earth exhibition 65–66

P
Patagonia 2, 11–12, 13, 17
Pollination 31
Powlesland, Paul 10–11
publishing, Nature's role in 63

R
Rathlin Island civic assembly 56
Raworth, Kate 66, 67
rewilding 12–13
Rights of Nature 8–11
river catchment partnerships 57–58
rivers 10, 18, 33, 56–58

Rose, Dr Juliet 35, 41–44
Royle, Javvy M. 50–52

S
Sagrada Familia, Barcelona 62
Sonic the dog 9, 36
Sounds Right music initiative 64
Spencer, Octavia 68, 71, 72
sustainability conferences 73
sustainability directors 71

U
United Nations General Assembly 73
University of Derby, *Nature Connected
    Communities Handbook* 5
Usk Catchment Partnership 57–58

V
volunteer groups 47–50

W
Well-being of Future Generations
    (Wales) Act 58–59
Whanganui river, New Zealand 10,
    18, 56–57
What would Nature say? 38–39
Whitehead, Lettie Pate 80, 81
willow 45, 49–50
Wilson, Grant 10
World Wide Fund for Nature, Living
    Planet Report 2
Wright, Amy 8
Wye river, UK 58

Y
Yamuna river, India 33